PERSPECTIVES

An Intermediate Reader

PERSPECTIVES
An Intermediate Reader

Len Fox

*Brooklyn College of the
City University of New York*

HARCOURT BRACE JOVANOVICH, PUBLISHERS
San Diego   New York   Chicago   Atlanta   Washington, D.C.
London   Sydney   Toronto

ISBN: 0-15-570486-9

Library of Congress Catalog Card Number: 79-91073

Printed in the United States of America

Dedicated to two very fine, warm, accepting parents,
Irving and Ruth Fox

PREFACE

When I first began to work on an intermediate-level reader for students of English as a second language, I wanted to choose readings that would not only allow students to practice English but would also teach them something about life in the United States. The result—drawn largely from magazine articles that deal with such subjects as immigrants, old age, education, housing, the media, and popular culture—is, I hope, an accurate picture of life in this country, according to the different perspectives of the authors of the articles. In addition, because the themes presented are of universal concern, the articles should stimulate ESL students to discuss how these areas of life are dealt with in their own cultures. In the process, besides learning English, the students will have the opportunity to think and learn about life in the United States, in their native country, and in the countries of their classmates.

In the following paragraphs are suggestions for making the best use of some of the elements of the text.

VOCABULARY

The original articles were shortened and simplified, using the two thousand words from Michael West's *General Service List* as a guide. A few more difficult words, explained in the margin, are included, not more frequently than one every three or four lines. The syntax was occasionally simplified but usually left as it was in the original articles. A list of all words used in the readings is included at the end.

PICTURES AND PREREADING DISCUSSION

At the beginning of each article is a picture related to the following
text. The instructor might ask students to describe the picture and tell
how they feel about it. The class can briefly discuss some ideas related
to the article before reading. For example, in the case of "The New
Immigrants," the instructor might ask, "Would you like to emigrate?
Why?" "Do you know anyone who emigrated? Why did he or she do
this?"

USEFUL WORDS AND EXPRESSIONS

Following each article are lists of words and expressions used in the
preceding text. The lists include all the words used in the subsequent
exercises, "Vocabulary" and "Common Expressions." If some of these
words are unfamiliar, students should review the indicated paragraphs
in order to be able to do the vocabulary and common-expressions
exercises.

READING COMPREHENSION EXERCISE

The first thing that students should ask themselves after reading a text
is "Have I understood what I have just read?" Thus the first question
in this exercise—"What is the main idea of the article?"—will show
whether students really have understood what the article was about. It
is important for instructors to explain that "main idea" does not mean
specific points mentioned in the text ("details") but the overall
meaning of the text. If students can't immediately answer other
reading-comprehension questions, they should skim the article and
reread specific paragraphs for the answers.

VOCABULARY DEVELOPMENT

The purpose of Exercises II–VI (Vocabulary, Prepositions, Common
Expressions, Definite/Indefinite Articles, Word Forms) is to allow
students, through repetition, to concentrate on and better learn some
of the important vocabulary and expressions used in the texts. ESL
students have particular difficulty in learning the use of prepositions,
articles, and word forms. It seems unfortunate that many ESL reading
texts do not include frequent exercises in these three areas.

COMMUNICATION EXERCISES

Values Discussion

Ideally, this exercise should be done in small groups of three or four students so that each student in the class gets a chance to speak. The goal of the exercise is to allow students to express their feelings and opinions about questions raised in the texts. There is no "correct" answer to these questions. In fact, in every question students have the opportunity to say whatever they want. To do the exercise, students should first be given about ten minutes to think about and answer the questions on their own. Then, beginning with question 1, or another question that a student may find more interesting, each student in the group will explain his or her reasons for choosing an answer. The group will probably not have time to discuss all the questions together; they can choose the ones they find most interesting.

Roleplaying

According to the roleplaying situation selected, students will be in pairs, groups of three or four, or all together as a class. Students should take about five minutes to plan what they are going to say before they begin to play the roles. The instructor and an advanced student might give a demonstration to begin this activity, or the instructor might choose a few of the better students to act in front of the class. The students could be asked to write up a dialogue or a play after they complete this activity.

For Discussion and Composition

After completing the values discussion and roleplaying exercises (although the instructor might choose to do just one of these exercises), the students should be prepared to write a short essay in response to one of the items in this exercise, since the ideas dealt with here are related to the previous exercises. For example, one values-discussion question is "What is the best reason to emigrate?"; a roleplaying situation "Nikki and Theodosios Kaffas are talking about why they are leaving Greece"; a composition question: "Why do people decide to emigrate to the United States?" One way to present this activity would be for the instructor, working with the whole class, to make a list of some ideas that could be used to answer a particular question. Students could then be allowed to answer in writing the essay that the teacher has outlined on the board. They could, of course, choose another question, if they prefer to prepare an outline themselves.

I wish to express my gratitude to my friends and colleagues Ginny Fox, Gloria Gallingane, Lily Kapili, and Harvey Nadler for commenting on early versions of this book. Thanks also to Shirley W. Braun, Marcia Cohen, and Clarice Kaltinick for their suggestions. I am indebted to Robert Oprandy and Pat Tirone for introducing me to values-clarification exercises. Ms. Audrey Forbes of *U.S. News & World Report* was exceptionally helpful to me. Finally, many thanks to William A. Pullin of Harcourt Brace Jovanovich, whose suggestions greatly improved the book and who was very patient with a person struggling to be a father, a teacher, and a textbook writer all at the same time.

Len Fox

CONTENTS

MEN AND WOMEN

LIFE IN CITIES

THE MEDIA

OLDER FOLKS

THE NEW IMMIGRANTS:* STILL THE PROMISED LAND?

Many people around the world are dissatisfied with their living conditions. They suffer from poverty, discrimination,° lack of **unfair treatment** *education, lack of job opportunities, lack of freedom, etc.° One way to* **and other things** *try to solve these problems is to move to another country. This doesn't necessarily mean that their problems will be solved. In fact, they will encounter° many new problems upon arriving in a new country, such* **meet** *as having to learn a new language, getting used to new customs, etc. Nevertheless, people continue to emigrate.° One of their most common* **leave their countries** *destinations is the United States.*

1. It is hard. It is hard to turn the key and lock the door. Hard to leave, probably forever, the little white house in the Peloponnesian town of Argos. The little house was given to Nikki Kaffas when she married Theodosios twelve years ago, and the tears come to her eyes as she
5   speaks of "the wonderful garden and the birds that sing all day. Now we must leave it all behind. But they tell me America is a nice place." Theodosios Kaffas is determined to make it so.° A barber who had to go   **that way** out of business, a restaurant cook who couldn't earn more than $300 a month, he has dreamed of going to America ever since he was a boy.
10 Now he is 36. "Argos is a good place for those who own fields and orange trees." says Kaffas, "but the workers are better paid in America. I want a better life for my family. I want to educate my children."

*people who move into a new country

Adapted by permission from *Time*, The Weekly Newsmagazine; Copyright Time Inc. 1976.

2. Victor Valles Solán, too, is greatly concerned about his children.
He has five of them, and in Cuba, where he once had a small steel
15 factory, he began to feel that they were becoming slaves of the state.
"We were allowed only one liter of fresh milk every other day," says
Valles, 46, "but what is more important is that every day the children
learned Communist ideas in the schools and going to church was never
talked about. I realize that I am going to the United States with many
20 illusions,° but for me your country is the place on earth where | false ideas
democracy is strongest."

3. Dr. Brian Pethica already knows the U.S. well, and he has no
problems, political or financial. Now 49, a chemist at the Unilever
Company in Port Sunlight, near Liverpool, Pethica has been crossing
25 the Atlantic at least once° a year since 1958, and he likes his job. But he | one time
wants to teach. He says, "The university system in England seems
somehow less open. In the U.S. there are many different kinds of
schools, which allows you to educate everyone as far as he can go. That
opportunity to have a richer life is an American quality."

30 **4.** Last week, these voyagers° all left for America, just in time to | travelers
celebrate° their first July 4 holiday. The Kaffases, with their two | do something to show
children of 11 and 8, were going to Philadelphia, where Nikki's brother | a day is important
hopes to find Theodosios work in a restaurant. Victor Valles Solán
took his family to Melrose Park, Illinois, where he has a job in a
35 factory. Dr. Pethica was going to Potsdam, New York, where he will
become dean° of the school of arts and sciences at Clarkson College. | head of a school

5. These are just a few of the new immigrants who today are entering
America. Their goals° are somewhat different from those of earlier | objectives
immigrants. Political problems are still an important cause of
40 immigration, but religious problems are no longer° a major cause. The | **no**...not any more
new immigrants do occasionally talk of getting rich, but they know
this is no longer a land of gold rushes and oil discoveries. Yet they do
see in America something that many Americans take for granted° or | **take**...do not
even forget they possess—freedom. That means not only freedom from | appreciate
45 discrimination and hunger but also from unbreakable social class
systems and ignorance.° To many, America is still the promised land. | lack of education
The newcomers find out soon enough that the United States too has its | dislike for a group of
share of poverty and prejudice,° but in their eyes it is nevertheless a | people
kind of Utopia.° | a perfect place

Useful Words and Expressions

introduction	living conditions
immigrants	suffer
dissatisfied	poverty

discrimination
lack of freedom
emigrate
new language
customs
paragraph 1
  lock the door
  leave
  tears
  go out of business
  earn
  ever since he was a boy
  own fields
  workers
  better paid
paragraph 2
  be concerned about
    something
  slaves
  allowed
  every other day
  Communist ideas
  schools
  church
  illusions
  democracy
paragraph 3
  problems

political
financial
at least
university system
less open
educate
as far as
opportunity
paragraph 4
  left
  in time
  July 4 holiday
  work
  restaurant
  factory
  college
paragraph 5
  goals
  somewhat different
  religious
  no longer
  getting rich
  take for granted
  freedom
  social class systems
  find out
  nevertheless

•   •   •   •   •E•X•E•R•C•I•S•E•S•   •   •   •   •

I READING COMPREHENSION

1. What is the main idea of the article?
    a. It is hard to emigrate to another country.
    b. The university system in England is less open.
    c. Many people emigrate to the United States to try to find a better life.

2. Why is Theodosios Kaffas emigrating?
    a. He wants to be a barber.
    b. The workers are better paid in America.
    c. He doesn't like his house.

3. What did Victor Valles most dislike about Cuba?
   a. Every day his children learned Communist ideas.
   b. He lost his steel factory.
   c. His family didn't have enough food.

4. Mr. Valles says, "I realize that I am going to the United States with many illusions." The word *illusions* means:
   a. false or untrue ideas
   b. hopes
   c. disappointments

5. How is the university system in the United States compared to that of England?
   a. It is less open.
   b. It is more open.
   c. It is the same.

6. How are the goals of modern immigrants different from those of earlier immigrants?
   a. They want a better life.
   b. They don't have political problems.
   c. Not so many have religious problems.

7. How is the United States different from many other countries?
   a. It does not have unbreakable social class systems.
   b. There is no poverty and prejudice.
   c. Everyone can get rich.

8. In paragraphs 1, 2, and 3:
   a. Life in the United States is discussed.
   b. The stories of three typical immigrants are told.
   c. Conditions in Greece are discussed.

II VOCABULARY

From the list of words below, choose the correct word for each blank space. Use each word only once.

illusions	left	nevertheless
slaves	tears	earn
allowed	lock	concerned
somewhat	system	own

1. It is hard to turn the key and _____ the door.
2. The _____ come to Nikki's eyes as she speaks of "the wonderful garden and the birds that sing all day."
3. A restaurant cook who couldn't _____ more than $300 a month, Theodosios has dreamed of going to America ever since he was a little boy.

4. Victor Valles Solán is greatly _____ about his children.
5. He began to feel that they were becoming _____ of the state.
6, "I realize that I am going to the United States with many _____."
7. "The university _____ in England seems somehow less open."
8. Last week, these voyagers all _____ for America.
9. Their goals are _____ different from those of earlier immigrants.
10. The newcomers find out that the United States has its share of poverty and prejudice, but to their eyes it is _____ a kind of Utopia.

III   PREPOSITIONS

Fill in the correct preposition for each blank space.

1. The little house was given _____ Nikki Kaffas when she married Theodosios twelve years ago.
2. "Argos is a good place _____ those who own fields and orange trees."
3. Victor Valles Solán is greatly concerned _____ his children.
4. He has five _____ them and he began to feel that they were becoming slaves _____ the state.
5. Going _____ church was never talked _____.
6. Now 49, a chemist _____ the Unilever Company _____ Port Sunlight, Pethica has been crossing the Atlantic _____ least once a year _____ 1958.
7. The Kaffasses, _____ their two children _____ 11 and 8, were going _____ Philadelphia.
8. Victor Valles Solán took his family _____ Melrose Park, Illinois, where he has a job _____ a factory.

IV   COMMON EXPRESSIONS

Choose the correct expression for each blank space.

ever since	at least	find out
social class	no longer	getting rich
out of business	every other day	as far as
in time	take for granted	better paid

1. A barber who had to go _____, Kaffas has dreamed of going to America ever since he was a boy.
2. "We were allowed only one liter of fresh milk _____."
3. Pethica has been crossing the Atlantic _____ once a year since 1958.
4. "In the U.S. there are many different kinds of schools, which allows you to educate everyone _____ he can go."
5. Last week, these voyagers all left for America, just _____ to celebrate their first July 4 holiday.
6. Religious problems are _____ a major cause of immigration.

7. The new immigrants do occasionally talk of _____.
8. They see in America something that many Americans _____.
9. They see not only freedom from discrimination and hunger but also from unbreakable _____ systems.
10. The newcomers _____ soon enough that the United States too has its share of poverty and prejudice.

V DEFINITE/INDEFINITE ARTICLES

Use *a/an* or *the* where needed. If no article is needed, write an X in the blank space.

These are just a few of _____ new immigrants who today are entering _____ America.. Their goals are somewhat different from those of _____ earlier immigrants. _____ political problems are still _____ important cause of _____ immigration, but _____ religious problems are no longer _____ major cause. _____ new immigrants do occasionally talk of getting rich, but they know this is no longer _____ land of _____ gold rushes and _____ oil discoveries. Yet they do see in _____ America something that _____ many Americans take for granted or even forget they possess— _____ freedom.

VI WORD FORMS

	verbs	nouns	adjectives and participles	adverbs
A.	discriminate	discrimination	discriminatory	
B.	educate	education	educational	educationally
			educated	
C.	possess	possession	possessive	possessively
D.	differ	difference	different	differently
E.	marry	marriage	married	
F.		politics	political	politically
G.	strengthen	strength	strong	strongly
H.	systemize	system	systematic	systematically

Use the correct word in the sentences below.

A. discriminate, discrimination, discriminatory
   1. In many countries, there is _____ against women.
   2. Employers _____ against women by offering them lower salaries.
   3. These _____ practices should be stopped.
B. educate, education, educational, educated, educationally
   1. A good _____ can help you find a good job.
   2. Teachers try to _____ their students.
   3. Dr. Johnson is an _____ man.

4. It is _____ harmful to have too many students in a class.
5. I saw an excellent _____ film yesterday.

C. possess, possession, possessive, possessively
1. That child will never share her toys; she is very _____.
2. She holds on to her toys very _____.
3. Very few people _____ all that they want.
4. Many people spend too much money to acquire _____ that they don't need.

D. differ, difference, different, differently
1. John _____ from his brother a great deal.
2. They have very _____ personalities.
3. The _____ between them is really remarkable.
4. They think _____.

E. marry, marriage, married
1. It is easy to get _____, but not so easy to have a good _____ .
2. It is unwise to _____ at a very young age.

F. politics, political, politically
1. John is interested in _____.
2. _____, he tends to be rather conservative.
3. I disagree with many of his _____ ideas.

G. strengthen, strength, strong, strongly
1. There was _____ opposition to Bob's plan.
2. The _____ of the opposition was surprising.
3. Even Jim, a good friend of Bob's, was _____ opposed to it.
4. Perhaps Bob could _____ the plan if he worked on it some more.

H. systematize, system, systematic, systematically
1. There is a good filing _____ in this office.
2. It was _____ by Mr. Jones' secretary.
3. She is very _____.
4. She _____ files everything that comes into the office.

VII   VALUES DISCUSSION

Answer the following questions. Then discuss your answers with your classmates.

1. How do you feel about emigrating?
   a. It is usually a good thing to do.
   b. It is usually not a good thing to do.
   c. People often do it and then regret it.
   d. other

2. What is the best reason to emigrate?
   a. You are unhappy with the political system of your native country.
   b. You are unhappy with the system of education.
   c. You don't have good job opportunities.
   d. other

3. What is the worst problem immigrants face in a new country?
   a. the new language
   b. the new customs
   c. missing their native country (feeling homesick)
   d. other

4. Under what circumstances would you advise someone to emigrate?
   a. The person can't find a good job.
   b. The person is afraid of being put in jail for political reasons.
   c. The person is bored with life in his or her country.
   d. other

5. What is the best thing about life in the United States?
   a. freedom of speech
   b. the high standard of living
   c. job opportunities
   d. other

6. What do you think immigrants miss most about their native country?
   a. the language
   b. the customs
   c. their friends
   d. other

7. What would you need in order to be happy in another country?
   a. money
   b. friends
   c. a good job
   d. other

8. The Kaffases had a nice house and lived in a nice town in Greece. How do you feel about their leaving Greece?
   a. It was a wise decision.
   b. They should have stayed in Greece.
   c. They may be sorry.
   d. other

9. Dr. Pethica wanted to teach in an "open" university system (where everyone can be educated as far as he or she can go). How do you feel about such an open system?
   a. It is good.
   b. It is bad.
   c. It is sometimes good.
   d. other

VIII   ROLEPLAYING

Choose one of the following situations to act out.

1. Nikki and Theodosios Kaffas are talking about why they are leaving Greece and going to the United States.

2. Victor Valles is explaining to one (or two or three) of his children why they are going to leave Cuba.
3. Dr. Pethica is explaining to another chemist in his company why he is going to the United States.
4. Two immigrants who have just arrived in the United States are discussing their feelings about being here (what they like and dislike).
5. An immigrant is explaining to an American the advantages and disadvantages of being in the United States.
6. An immigrant has gone back to visit his or her native country and is telling a friend (or group of friends) there about the advantages and disadvantages of life in the United States.
7. A husband (you choose in which country) is trying to convince his wife that they should emigrate to the United States. The wife wants to stay in her native country (or vice versa, the wife is trying to convince the husband to emigrate).
8. After they have emigrated to the United States, a husband is trying to convince his wife that they have made a mistake and should go back to their native country (or vice versa, the wife is trying to convince the husband to go back).
9. An American politician is speaking to a reporter or group of reporters (which can be the whole class) about what the United States does for immigrants in this country. The reporter(s) can then ask questions.

IX   FOR DISCUSSION AND COMPOSITION

Choose one of the following to discuss or write about.

1. Why do people decide to emigrate to the United States?
2. What are some difficulties that people have when they emigrate to the United States?
3. What is the worst problem that immigrants have in the United States? Why?
4. Describe one problem in a specific country that causes people to emigrate (such as the political situation, poverty, unemployment, low pay).
5. Describe the experience of a particular family that decided to emigrate to the United States. (You may choose to describe your own family if they are immigrants.) Why did they emigrate? What was life in the United States like for them at first? What is it like now?
6. Compare the advantages of living in the United States to those of living in another country (for example, in your native country).
7. What could be done in the United States to make life easier for immigrants.
8. Describe a particular group of immigrants living in the United States. Where do they live? What do they do? How do they feel about living in the United States?
9. Describe the situation of "illegal aliens" in the United States. Should these people be forced to leave the United States? Should they be allowed to become citizens?
10. Discuss the advantages and disadvantages of an "open" education system, where everyone can be educated as far as he or she can go.

ADULT*STUDENTS GIVE NEW LIFE TO EDUCATION

Schools used to be considered places to prepare young people for life. After their education was finished, they were supposed to be ready to go out into the real world. But many adults these days are coming back to "schools of continuing education" and "centers of lifelong learning." They feel that one's education is never really ended, because one is never too old to learn.

1.   A fast-growing number of older students are helping schools that once ignored° their needs. Filling empty seats in classrooms from Maine to Hawaii, students who are twenty-five and older are having a great effect on all fields of higher education. In all, there are 17 million
5   of them. Programs include courses offered by high schools, local governments, federal agencies,° and private groups. But it is at the college level where effects are the greatest. Educators say the registration° of older students is caused by a growing feeling of Americans that education is a lifelong effort. It has provided new
10   variety as well as needed dollars to schools traditionally° intended for students in their teens and early twenties.

2.   As the number of younger students has stopped growing, the enrollment° of older ones has quickly increased—more than doubling since 1970. About a third of the nation's college students are twenty-five
15   or over, mostly enrolled in part-time programs that schools can offer profitably. By 1980, these older students are expected to include 40

°paid no attention to

°departments

°becoming a student in a school

°according to past customs

°joining a school

*a mature, older person

Adapted from *U.S. News & World Report* (March 28, 1977).

percent of the campus° population, according to Census Bureau estimates.° Olin Cook, director of higher education for the state of Arkansas, says: "Adult education will keep the classes filled and the
20 bills paid."

college
judgments about size, number

3. Teachers say that there has been a definite° effect on classrooms and course work. Older students are described as more serious and mature, frequently more demanding of instructors, and more willing to contribute personal experiences to discussions. "Older people make
25 very good students," says L. Jay Oliva, vice president for academic planning° and services at New York University. "They realize that they are here to do X, Y, Z, and they want the professor to teach them that. They are very attentive and concerned." A Michigan educator, Elinor P. Waters, believes that the presence of older students on campus "will
30 take us a step closer to the real world; there will be fewer irrelevant° courses and more practical ones."

clear

academic...planning of classes

unrelated to the real world

4. Why do adults want to reenter academic life? School administrators° say high unemployment is one of the biggest reasons, forcing many Americans to develop new skills. In addition a large number of
35 women who left school to raise families or who want jobs that require° a college diploma are going back to school. College graduates are returning for second degrees to start new careers. And there are thousands of retired persons who are seeking° good use of their free time

directors

demand

looking for

40 5. Many students feel that they are better prepared for learning than they were when they were younger. For example, Jane Pirozzolo, who will soon receive a degree in English from Boston University, graduated° from junior college in 1967 and has worked as a secretary since then. Explaining her decision to return to school, she says: "I felt
45 overqualified° for the jobs I was doing, and they were becoming increasingly boring.° Now I feel I can understand what the professor wants, and I can study and read better than I could ten years ago. I feel like I'm one step ahead of the younger students."

got a college degree

too qualified
uninteresting

6. Courses popular among adults are federal income tax trends,° law,
50 business English, and principles of real estate. Self-improvement studies go from such classes as European cooking and the study of wines to tennis, backpacking,° belly dancing, plant care, and meditation for relaxation. More traditional courses leading to college degrees may include philosophy, psychology, history, economics, and
55 science. Most college catalogues° list at least 200 separate courses.

general direction of development

carrying one's supplies while camping

books that show what is available

7. A few schools have made little effort to compete for older students. "Many older faculty members feel very comfortable with the ways of the past," says J. Christopher Gemmell, an official of the American

Association of State Colleges and Universities. He adds that some
60 teachers are frightened by this rush of people their own age who have
been out in the real world suddenly moving into their territory.
Sometimes their classroom theories° are questioned by adults who are | ideas
used to practicality and results.

8. Despite° these objections, most educators are convinced that the | in spite of, even with
65 growth of adult learning is an important change in American
education. Proof of the great interest in adult education is the action
being taken to attract adult students:
—San Francisco's Golden Gate University, located near the city's
financial district, has doubled its enrollment to 9,000 in five years by
70 offering classes in business, public service, and law that interest | people with a profession: lawyers, doctors, etc.
professionals.°
—Adelphi University on New York's Long Island offers courses to
commuters° on four railroad lines during rush hours. Lectures and | people who travel to work and back home
course work take place in train cars, where about 125 students have
75 earned master's degrees in business administration since the program
started in 1971.
—The College of Lifelong Learning at Wayne State University in
Detroit runs a "Week-end College" for about 3,000 adult undergradu-
ates.° The students watch lectures on television and attend one class in | students who haven't yet graduated from college
80 their neighborhood during the week, and then study at the downtown
college campus on Saturday and Sunday.

9. In the future, says Allan W. Ostar, executive director of the
American Association of State Colleges and Universities, schools will
change their programs and create new ones for their adult students. He
85 believes that schools will have to "work much harder in all they do
because they are dealing with a different consumer,° a far more | someone who buys, consumes
demanding consumer. When you're paying for your education
yourself, your level of expectation rises significantly."° | a lot, noticeably

10. Also, both young and old students seem to be enjoying the
90 appearance of older and more experienced classmates. "It's good for the
adults to find out that college students are not bad kids or nuts° and are | crazy people
probably more mature than they were at that age," says Fritz
McCameron, dean of continuing education at Louisiana State
University. "And it has shown the kids that adults are not over the | **over**...too old to be useful
95 hill,° that there is hope for you if you're over 35."

Copyright 1977 U.S. News & World Report, Inc.

Useful Words and Expressions

introduction   life
  prepare   education

adults
coming back
paragraph 1
ignored
needs
empty seats
having a great effect
federal agencies
the college level
as well as
paragraph 2
part time programs
40 percent
estimates
paragraph 3
a definite effect
serious
personal experiences
the real world
irrelevant
practical
paragraph 4
unemployment
jobs
require
college diploma
new careers
retired
free time

paragraph 5
better prepared
one step ahead
paragraph 6
income tax
law
English
real estate
self improvement
at least
paragraph 7
made little effort
frightened
theories
paragraph 8
despite
objections
educators
convinced
paragraph 9
in the future
change
dealing with
consumer
expectation
rises
paragraph 10
find out
over the hill

• • • • •E•X•E•R•C•I•S•E•S• • • • •

I READING COMPREHENSION

1. What is the main idea of the article?
    a. Education is a lifelong effort.
    b. A large number of adults are going back to school.
    c. Older students are more serious.

2. According to the article, how many of the nation's college students are twenty-five or over?
    a. about a third
    b. 40 percent
    c. one-half

3. According to L. Jay Oliva
   a. Older students don't know what they want.
   b. Older students are not attentive.
   c. Older students know what they want from their professors.

4. Which paragraph gives several reasons why older people want to go back to school?
   a. paragraph 4
   b. paragraph 3
   c. paragraph 1

5. Jane Pirozzolo
   a. was not qualified for the jobs she was doing
   b. finds school more difficult than before
   c. finds school less difficult than before

6. In paragraph 6, *traditional* means
   a. according to past customs
   b. new
   c. necessary

7. The author of this article
   a. feels that adult students have a positive effect on education
   b. feels that adult students have a negative effect on education
   c. feels that young people do not want adult students in their classes

8. Put in the correct order
   a. For example, Jane Pirozzolo, who will receive a degree in English from Boston University this spring, graduated from junior college in 1967 and has worked as a secretary since then.
   b. Many students feel they are better prepared for learning than when they were younger.
   c. Explaining her decision to return to school, she says, "I felt overqualified for the jobs I was doing."

II   VOCABULARY

From the list of words below, choose the correct word for each blank space. Use each word only once.

theories	ignored	rises
require	definite	irrelevant
agencies	empty	despite
estimates	consumer	unemployment

1. A fast-growing number of older students are helping schools that once _____ their needs.

2. Filling _____ seats in classrooms from Maine to Hawaii, students who are twenty-five and older are having a great effect on all fields of higher education.

3. By 1980, these older students are expected to include 40 percent of the campus population, according to Census Bureau _____.

4. Teachers say that there has been a _____ effect on classrooms and course work.

5. There will be fewer _____ courses and more practical ones.

6. School administrators say high _____ is one of the biggest reasons why adults want to reenter academic life.

7. A large number of women want jobs that _____ a college diploma.

8. Sometimes the professors' classroom _____ are questioned by adults who are used to practicality and results.

9. _____ these objections, most educators are convinced that the growth of adult learning is an important change.

10. Schools will have to work much harder because they are dealing with a different _____, a far more demanding one.

III   PREPOSITIONS

Fill in the correct preposition for each blank space.

1. Filling empty seats _____ classrooms _____ Maine _____ Hawaii, students who are twenty-five and older are having a great effect _____ all fields _____ higher education.

2. The older students have provided new variety as well as needed dollars _____ schools traditionally intended _____ students _____ their teens and early twenties.

3. By 1980, these older students are expected to include 40 percent _____ the campus population, according _____ Census Bureau estimates.

4. Elinor P. Waters believes that the presence _____ older students _____ campus "will take us a step closer _____ the real world."

5. Some teachers are frightened _____ this rush_____ people their own age who have been out _____ the real world suddenly moving _____ their territory.

6. San Francisco's Golden Gate University, located _____ the city's financial district, has doubled its enrollment _____ 9,000 _____ five years _____ offering classes _____ business, public service, and law.

7. Adelphi University _____ New York's Long Island offers courses _____ commuters _____ four railroad lines _____ rush hours.

8. The College _____ Lifelong Learning _____ Wayne State University _____ Detroit runs a "Week-end College" _____ about 3,000 adult undergraduates.

IV   COMMON EXPRESSIONS

Choose the correct expression for each blank space.

in the future	made little effort	part-time
real world	as well as	dealing with
having a great effect	at least	personal experiences
find out	college diploma	over the hill

1. Students who are twenty-five and older are _____ on all fields of higher education.
2. It has provided new variety _____ needed dollars to schools traditionally intended for students in their teens and early twenties.
3. The older students are mostly enrolled in _____ programs that schools can offer profitably.
4. Older students are more willing to contribute _____ to discussions.
5. The presence of older students on campus will take us a step closer to the _____ .
6. Most college catalogues list _____ 200 separate courses.
7. A few schools have _____ to compete for older students.
8. _____, schools will change their programs and create new ones for their adult students.
9. Schools will have to work much harder because they are _____ a different consumer.
10. It's good for the adults to _____ that college students are not bad kids or nuts.

V   DEFINITE/INDEFINITE ARTICLES

Use *a/an* or *the* where needed. If no article is needed, write an X in the blank space.

In _____ future, says Allan W. Ostar, executive director of _____ American Association of State Colleges and Universities, _____ schools will change their programs and create new ones for their adult students. He believes that _____ schools will have to "work much harder in all they do because they are dealing with _____ different consumer, _____ far more demanding consumer. When you're paying for your education yourself, your level of _____ expectation rises significantly."

VI   WORD FORMS

| | | adjectives and | |
verbs	nouns	participles	adverbs
A. attract	attraction	attractive	attractively
B. need	necessity	necessary	necessarily
C.	effect	effective	effectively
D.	seriousness	serious	seriously
E. employ	employment	employed	
	unemployment	unemployed	
	employer		
	employee		

verbs	nouns	**adjectives and participles**	adverbs
F. interest	interest	interesting interested	interestingly
G. create	creation	creative	creatively
H. enjoy	enjoyment	enjoyable	enjoyably

Use the correct word in the sentences below.

A. attract, attraction, attractive, attractively
   1. Jane is wearing an _____ dress today.
   2. She always dresses very _____.
   3. The possibility of finding a good job _____ many people to New York City.
   4. In other words, job opportunities are one of the biggest _____ of New York City.

B. need, necessity, necessary, necessarily
   1. A college degree is a _____ for many jobs today.
   2. Students _____ to learn skills in college that they will use later on in life.
   3. Getting a college degree, however, does not _____ mean you will find a job.
   4. Sometimes it is _____ to know the right people in order to get a job.

C. effect, effective, effectively
   1. Sam spoke very _____ at the meeting.
   2. His speech was very _____.
   3. He hopes that the program he is suggesting will have a positive _____.

D. seriousness, serious, seriously
   1. John is always _____.
   2. He speaks _____ about everything.
   3. Sometimes people get a little tired of his _____.

E. employ, employment, unemployment, employer, employee, employed, unemployed
   1. My _____ promised to give me a raise next year.
   2. He says I am a very good _____.
   3. Jim was fired last week; now he is _____.
   4. He plans to collect _____ insurance.
   5. Most people are _____ in the United States.
   6. We are fortunate to have a relatively high rate of _____.
   7. The government _____ a lot of people in this country.

F. interest, interest, interesting, interested, interestingly
   1. My sociology class _____ me a great deal.
   2. I find it _____.
   3. George, on the other hand, is not _____ in it.

4. He doesn't think the teacher lectures _____.
5. He has no _____ in the readings either.

G. create, creation, creative, creatively
   1. Artists are _____ people.
   2. People come to museums to admire artists' _____.
   3. Artists see things _____.
   4. It is a great gift to be able to _____ something new, different, and interesting to others.

H. enjoy, enjoyment, enjoyable, enjoyably
   1. Jane says her visit to New York was very _____.
   2. She spent her time _____.
   3. She especially _____ her walk around Brooklyn Heights.
   4. New York City is a good place to go for _____.

VII   VALUES DISCUSSION

Answer the following questions. Then discuss your answers with your classmates.

1. What is the best reason for adults to go back to school?
   a. All their friends are doing it.
   b. They have nothing else to do with their free time.
   c. They need to do it in order to get a better job.
   d. other

2. What is the greatest advantage of getting an education?
   a. You can get a better job.
   b. You are a more interesting person.
   c. You can help to improve the world.
   c. other

3. How do most adults feel about going back to school?
   a. It is easier than when they were younger.
   b. It was easier when they were younger.
   c. They are ashamed because school is for kids.
   d. other

4. How do most teachers feel about teaching adults?
   a. They like it more than teaching younger people.
   b. They like teaching young people more.
   c. They are afraid of the adults.
   d. other

5. How do you feel about having adults and younger people in the same class?
   a. It is a good idea.
   b. It is a bad idea.
   c. It makes things more difficult for the teacher.
   d. other

6. As an adult going back to school, what course would you most want to take?
    a. income tax
    b. cooking
    c. foreign languages
    d. other

7. As a young student, how would you feel about having adults in your class?
    a. I would like it.
    b. I wouldn't like it.
    c. I would be afraid to speak.
    d. other

8. As an adult, how would you feel about being in a class with younger students?
    a. I would like it.
    b. I wouldn't like it.
    c. I wouldn't be able to speak honestly.
    d. other

9. What is the best thing about adult students?
    a. They work harder.
    b. They have interesting experiences to talk about.
    c. They know what they want.
    d. other

10. What is the overall effect of having adult students in schools?
    a. good
    b. bad
    c. good for the schools, but bad for the teachers
    d. other

11. How do you feel about learning English in school?
    a. It is useful.
    b. It is not useful.
    c. It is useful only if you are going to live in an English speaking country.
    d. other

12. How do you feel about the English courses you have taken at school?
    a. They have been good.
    b. They haven't been good.
    c. I wasn't able to speak enough in class.
    d. other

VIII   ROLEPLAYING

Choose one of the following situations to act out.

1. A college administrator is telling one or a group of adults (which could be the whole class) why they should go back to school. The adult(s) will then ask questions about this.
2. A young person asks an adult student why he or she is going back to school. The adult student answers and then asks the younger student how he or she feels about having older students in class.
3. Two teachers are talking about having adult students in their classes. One likes it and the other doesn't.
4. An adult student is telling a college admissions counselor why he or she wants to go back to school.
5. A college administrator is telling a newspaper reporter why he or she is happy to have adult students at the college.
6. Two adults are discussing their main reason for going back to college. (It can be to get a better job, to enjoy their free time, to learn about a specific subject.)
7. Jane Pirozzolo is discussing with a friend why she feels better now that she is back in school.
8. Two young students are discussing their feelings about having adult students in their classes. One likes it and the other doesn't.
9. An adult student is telling a teacher that the course (psychology or literature, for example), is not practical enough (too theoretical).
10. An adult student is telling a friend about the Adelphi University course he or she is taking on the Long Island Railroad.
11. An adult student who wants to learn English is arguing with one who doesn't.
12. Two students are discussing what they like or dislike about their English class.

IX   FOR DISCUSSION AND COMPOSITION

Choose one of the following to discuss or write about.

1. Explain why adults are going back to school.
2. Why is it important to get a good education.
3. Compared to younger people, is it easier or more difficult for adults to be in school? Why?
4. Do you think it is easier to teach adults or young people? Why?
5. Is it good to have both adults and younger people in the same class? Why?
6. What are some specific courses that could be useful to adults? Why?
7. Discuss how the presence of older students affects a class.
8. As a younger person, how would you feel about having adults in your class?
9. As an adult, how would you feel about being in a class with younger students?
10. Discuss the good and bad parts of your own education.
11. Discuss the advantages of learning English.
12. What have you liked and/or disliked about the English classes you have taken?

DAY CARE
FOR THE ELDERLY*

In many countries, old people live with their families. In the United States, old people often live alone. Frequently, their children live far away from them and are not able to visit them very often. The lives of old people are sometimes lonely and unhappy. Many feel that they have no place in their society. The following text discusses one possible solution to this problem.

1. For four lonely years, Evelyn Jones of Rockford, Illinois, lived friendless and forgotten in one room of a cheap hotel. "I wasn't sick, but I was acting sick," the 78-year-old widow° says. "Every day was the same—I would just lie on my bed and maybe cook up some soup." Then, six months ago, she was invited to "The Brighter Side," Rockford's day care center° for the elderly. Every weekday morning since then, she has left her rundown° room to meet nine other old people in a church for a rich program of charity work,° trips, games, and—most important of all—friendly companionship.

woman whose husband is dead

day...place to stay during the day

in bad condition
charity...work to help poor people

2. Just a few years ago, there were few choices for the elderly between a normal life in their own homes and being totally confined° in nursing homes.° Many of them were sent to rest homes long before they needed full-time care. Others, like Mrs. Jones, were left to take care of themselves. But in 1971, the White House Conference° on Aging called

limited, locked up
nursing...places for old people to live

meeting to discuss a particular subject

*older people

15 for the development of alternatives° to care in nursing homes for old
people, and since then, government-supported day-care programs like
The Brighter Side have been developed in most big American cities.

3. "This represents a real alternative to the feared institution° and
makes old people believe they have not left the world of the living,"
20 says Alice Brophy, 64, director of New York City's Office for the Aging.
"They do well at the centers, and I hate it when people describe us as
elderly playpens.°" New York's 138 centers encourage continuing
contact for the aged with the community's life. The centers serve more
than 15,000 members, and volunteer workers° are always looking for
25 new ones. If someone does not show up at the center for several days in
a row, a worker at the center calls to make sure° all is well. And
although participation in the center is free, those who want to can pay
for their hot lunches.

4. No formal studies have been made of these centers for the elderly,
30 but government officials are enthusiastic.° In the future, the Public
Health Service will do a study to decide if the programs can receive
federal medicare money.° And the old people themselves are very happy
with the programs. "There is no way," says Evelyn Jones, smiling at
her new companions at The Brighter Side, "that I will ever go back to
35 spending my day with all those losers° at the hotel."

other choices

home for old people

enclosed place for a baby to play

volunteer...workers who are not paid

make...be certain

very interested

medicare...money from a national health care program

unhappy people (not formal English)

Useful Words and Expressions

introduction
   old people
   alone
   children
   far away
   unhappy
   solution
   problem
paragraph 1
   lonely
   acting sick
   widow
   the same
   lie
   day care center
   program
   most important of all
   companionship
paragraph 2
   a few years ago
   choices

normal life
nursing homes
full-time care
take care of themselves
called for
alternatives
day care programs
developed
paragraph 3
do well
describe
playpens
encourage
the aged
the community
serve
members
looking for
several days in a row
participation

paragraph 4
  government officials   no way
  enthusiastic   go back
  do a study   companions

• • • • •E•X•E•R•C•I•S•E•S• • • • • •

I READING COMPREHENSION

1. What is the main idea of the article?
   a. Day care centers may be able to receive federal medicare money.
   b. Day care centers can make life better for elderly people.
   c. Many old people in the United States are lonely.

2. What does Evelyn Jones say about herself in paragraph 1?
   a. "I was sick."
   b. "Every day was different."
   c. "I was acting sick."

3. According to paragraph 2, why did many old people have to go to nursing homes?
   a. They needed full-time care.
   b. They wanted to go there.
   c. They were sent there.

4. According to Alice Brophy (in paragraph 3)
   a. The centers are like elderly playpens.
   b. The old people do well at the day care centers.
   c. Old people like nursing institutions.

5. "*This* represents a real alternative to the feared institution." (paragraph 3) The word *this* means
   a. most big American cities
   b. rest homes
   c. day care programs

6. Which is *not* true?
   a. Evelyn has companions at The Brighter Side.
   b. Evelyn misses her friends at the hotel.
   c. Evelyn is happier than she was before.

7. Put the following sentences in the correct order.

a. Many of them were sent to rest homes long before they needed full-time care.
b. Just a few years ago, there were few choices for the elderly between a normal life in their own homes and being totally confined in nursing homes.
c. Others, like Mrs. Jones, were left to take care of themselves.

8. How does the writer of the article seem to feel about day care centers for the elderly?
   a. The writer approves of them.
   b. The writer disapproves of them.
   c. The writer thinks nursing homes are better.

II VOCABULARY

From the list of words below, choose the correct word for each blank space. Use each word only once.

program	lonely	lie
companions	widow	describe
encourage	enthusiastic	developed
serve	participation	choices

1. For four _____ years, Evelyn Jones lived friendless and forgotten in one room of a cheap hotel.
2. "I would just _____ on my bed and maybe cook up some soup."
3. Every weekday morning, she has left her rundown room for a rich _____ of charity work, trips, games, and companionship.
4. Just a few years ago, there were few _____ for the elderly.
5. Government-supported day care programs have been _____ in most big American cities.
6. "I hate it when people _____ us as elderly playpens."
7. The centers _____ continuing contact with the community.
8. Although _____ in the center is free, those who want to can pay for their hot lunches.
9. No formal studies have been made, but government officials are _____.
10. "There is no way," says Evelyn Jones, smiling at her new _____, "that I will go back to those losers at the hotel."

III PREPOSITIONS

Fill in the correct preposition for each blank space.

1. _____ four lonely years, Evelyn Jones _____ Rockford, Illinois, lived friendless and forgotten _____ one room _____ a cheap hotel.
2. Then, six months ago, she was invited _____ "The Brighter Side," Rockford's day care center _____ the elderly.

3. Just a few years ago, there were few choices _____ the elderly _____ a normal life _____ their own homes and being totally confined _____ nursing homes.
4. Many _____ them were sent _____ rest homes long before they needed full-time care.
5. _____ 1971, the White House Conference _____ Aging called _____ the development _____ alternatives _____ care _____ nursing homes.
6. They do well _____ the centers.
7. New York's 138 centers encourage continuing contact _____ the aged _____ the community's life.
8. "There is no way," says Evelyn Jones, smiling _____ her new companions, "that I will ever go back _____ spending my day _____ all those losers _____ the hotel."

IV COMMON EXPRESSIONS

Choose the correct expression for each blank space.

called for	no way	looking for
most important of all	a few	in a row
do well	take care of	full-time
the same	do a study	the aged

1. "Every day was _____—I would just lie on my bed and maybe cook up some soup."
2. She has been going to "The Brighter Side" for a rich program of charity work, trips, games, and—_____—friendly companionship.
3. Just _____ years ago, there were few choices for the elderly between a normal life in their own homes and being totally confined in nursing homes.
4. Many of them were sent to rest homes before they needed _____ care.
5. Others, like Mrs. Jones, were left to _____ themselves.
6. The old people _____ at the centers.
7. The centers encourage continuing contact for _____ with the community's life.
8. If someone does not show up at the center for several days _____ a worker calls to make sure all is well.
9. The Public Health Service will _____ to decide if the programs can receive federal medicare money.
10. "There is _____," says Evelyn Jones, "that I will ever go back to spending my day with all those losers at the hotel."

V DEFINITE/INDEFINITE ARTICLES

Use *a/an* or *the* where needed. If no article is needed, write an X in the blank space.

"These day care centers represent _____ real alternative to _____ feared institution and make _____ old people believe they have not left _____ world of _____ living," says Alice Brophy, 64, director of _____ New York City's Office for _____ Aging. "They do well at _____ centers, and I hate it when _____ people describe us as _____ elderly playpens." _____ New York's 138 centers encourage _____ continuing contact for _____ aged with _____ community's life. _____ centers serve more than _____ 15,000 members, and _____ volunteer workers are always looking for _____ new ones.

VI   WORD FORMS

verbs	nouns	adjectives and participles	adverbs
A. care	care	careful	carefully
	carelessness	careless	carelessly
B. fear	fear	afraid	fearlessly
		fearless	
C. live	life	living	
	liveliness	lively	
D. decide	decision	decisive	decisively
E. encourage	encouragement	encouraging	encouragingly
		encouraged	
F.	enthusiasm	enthusiastic	enthusiastically
G. free	freedom	free	freely
H. sicken	sickness	sick	
		sickening	sickeningly

Use the correct word form in the sentences below.

A. care, care, careful, careless, carefully, carelessly
1. Bob has many accidents; he is a very _____ driver.
2. He shouldn't drive so _____.
3. His wife always tells him to be more _____.
4. If he drove more _____, he wouldn't have so many accidents.
5. It is difficult to _____ for children.
6. Children need a lot of _____.

B. fear, fear, afraid, fearless, fearlessly
1. _____ of the dark is very common.
2. Children are especially _____ of the dark.
3. Many adults also _____ the dark.
4. The lion tamer was _____.
5. He walked into the lion's cage _____.

C. live, life, liveliness, living, lively
1. _____ in New York City is not easy.

2. Many people come to _____ in New York.
3. Mary has three _____ grandparents.
4. John is a _____ child.
5. His _____ sometimes gets him into trouble.

D. decide, decision, decisive, decisively
   1. It was difficult for me to _____ to move.
   2. That was a very difficult _____ to make.
   3. Sometimes it is difficult for me to be _____ about what I want to do.
   4. I don't always act very _____.

E. encourage, encouragement, encouraging, encouraged, encouragingly
   1. John's parents _____ him to go to college.
   2. They always speak to him _____ about going to college.
   3. Some of his friends say college is hard; he doesn't feel very _____ when he speaks to them.
   4. His grades in high school are good; that is _____.
   5. He needs a little more _____ before he can decide to go.

F. enthusiasm, enthusiastic, enthusiastically
   1. I feel _____ about going to Europe this summer.
   2. I haven't felt so much _____ about anything for some time.
   3. I am planning my trip _____.

G. free, freedom, free, freely
   1. People have _____ of speech in the United States.
   2. They can talk _____ about most subjects without fear of punishment.
   3. They are _____ to criticize the government if they want to.
   4. Many people in the world wish to _____ themselves from oppression.

H. sicken, sickness, sick, sickening, sickeningly
   1. Jim's childish behavior _____ me.
   2. His behavior is _____.
   3. I wish he weren't so _____ immature.
   4. If you go out without a coat, you could get _____.
   5. You could catch a serious _____ like that.

VII VALUES DISCUSSION

Answer the following questions. Then discuss your answers with your classmates.

1. Under what circumstances would you invite your aging parent to live with you?

a. only if he or she were not able to take care of himself or herself
b. only if it were not possible to send him or her to a nursing home
c. I would be glad to under any circumstances.
d. other

2. If you were old, where would you want to live?
   a. at home by myself
   b. with my family
   c. in a nursing home
   d. other

3. What is the greatest advantage of old age?
   a. You don't have to work.
   b. You understand things very well.
   c. You can enjoy life more.
   d. other

4. What is the greatest disadvantage of old age?
   a. You are going to die soon.
   b. You often get sick.
   c. Young people don't respect you.
   d. other

5. How will you feel when you are old?
   a. very good
   b. not good
   c. I don't know.
   d. other

6. What will make you happy in your old age?
   a. money
   b. enjoying my children
   c. having free time
   d. other

7. Until what age would you like to live?
   a. 60
   b. 70
   c. 80
   d. other

8. At what age would you like to retire (stop working)?
   a. 50
   b. 60
   c. 70
   d. other

9. What is the best activity for old people?
   a. talking with friends
   b. visiting their family
   c. watching T.V.
   d. other

10. How do you feel about old people?
    a. I admire them.
    b. I don't like them.
    c. I don't know any.
    d. other

11. Who should take care of old people?
    a. They should take care of themselves.
    b. their family
    c. the government
    d. other

12. What do old people need most?
    a. money
    b. love
    c. friends
    d. other

VIII ROLEPLAYING

Choose one of the following situations to act out.

1. Evelyn Jones is talking with another old person at The Brighter Side about why they enjoy this place.
2. Evelyn Jones is telling someone who lives at her hotel why he or she should go to The Brighter Side.
3. A volunteer worker at The Brighter Side is calling up a member to ask why he or she hasn't been there for a few days.
4. An old person is explaining to his or her child (son or daughter) why he or she doesn't want to live in a nursing home.
5. Two old people are discussing how they feel about living alone.
6. Two old people who are going to retire (stop working) are discussing their feelings about this.
7. An old person is speaking to his or her grandchild about the advantages and disadvantages of being old.
8. A politician is speaking to a reporter (or group of reporters, or group of old people, which can include the whole class) about what he or she plans to do for the elderly.
9. A husband and wife are talking about whether the wife's 70-year-old mother (or father) should come and live with them.

IX FOR DISCUSSION AND COMPOSITION

Choose one of the following to discuss or write about.

1. The development of day care centers is one possible way of improving the lives of old people in the United States. Discuss this and other ways of making life better for the elderly.
2. Why do many old people fear going to an institution for the elderly?
3. Many old people find that they don't know what to do with themselves after they retire from work. What can old people do to avoid this situation or to solve such a problem?
4. Why is life often difficult for old people?
5. Are there some advantages to old age? What are they?
6. Discuss the lives of old people in your native country. (Where do they live? Do they have a good life?)
7. Compare the lives of old people in your native country and in the United States.
8. Do you think you will enjoy old age? Why?
9. Describe the life of an old person that you know (for example, a grandfather, grandmother, friend). Is it a good life? Why?

YOUNG FOLKS

TRAINING
FOR REAL JOBS

Schools used to teach many subjects (for example, Latin and Greek)
that, although interesting, were not really necessary for success in the
real world. These days, many schools are developing programs that
teach practical subjects and prepare students for jobs in the real world.
v *In these programs, children go on trips to learn about different kinds of*
work and adults come to schools to speak about their jobs. This new
approach is called "career education."

1.   A new effort to help America's young people find and hold jobs is
being made in the nation's schools. Faced with a generation of
youngsters who have an increasingly difficult time getting hired,
educators are testing new methods° of preparing students for   ways
5. employment. Involved in° what is known as career education is a wide   **involved**...related to
variety of courses designed to show students how to find work and
satisfy an employer. Computers, on-the-job visits, and acting out work
situations in class are used to teach people skills from simple
bookkeeping to taking job interviews.° The method is midway between   **job**...meetings with
10 general school studies and vocational education, which provides   possible employers
training for a particular job. Much of the career education is included
in normal° classes that are taken by students starting with elementary usual, regular
school.°   **elementary**...the first
                                                                     six years of school
2.   "Vocational and back-to-basics° courses are also growing rapidly, a return to reading,
15 and that's fine with us," says Kenneth Hoyt, director of career   writing, and
                                                                     mathematics

Adapted from *U.S. News & World Report* (November 22, 1976).

education for the U.S. Office of Education in Washington, D.C. He observes, "What we're trying to do is show students how the three R's° and everything else they learn are useful in the big world outside of class. This approach is interesting a lot of kids who used to see no
20 point in school."

three...reading, writing, and arithmetic

3. To plan for an increased effort, 6,000 educators, business executives,° and labor leaders met in Houston to discuss future changes in career education. Showing the urgency° of the situation was a report that 19 percent of teenagers are unemployed at a time when more than
25 a million jobs are unfilled. Another finding at the conference: more than half of a group of seventeen-year-olds studied were unable to write a job application satisfactorily.

directors

importance

4. Among the most important projects° going on in career education: —Thousands of workers are going into schools, explaining what they
30 do and how students can get into their fields.
—Employers are giving schools up-to-date° information on job opportunities and qualifications to help young people prepare for careers.
—High schools and colleges are sending large numbers of pupils to
35 work part time in offices, shops, garages, and community centers as paid employees or volunteers.

works in progress

of the present time

5. Some projects are planned to make use of the real-life interests of young people. Animal-loving elementary school students, for example, in addition to learning about animals, are learning about selling by
40 taking trips to pet stores. Elsewhere, children interested in machines are visited by a motorcycle mechanic who explains how he had to spend $400 for a bookkeeper to keep his accounts because he didn't learn enough mathematics in school. In some schools students are acting out working conditions. Classes from North Little Rock,
45 Arkansas, to Scio, New York, practice economics and mathematics by operating small stores and banks in school, using play or even real money.

6. These and other projects are being organized by career-education specialists in 9,200 of the nation's 16,700 school districts—often with
50 help from teachers, business people, and local leaders. Says Mr. Hoyt, "This way of teaching is getting more and more popular with everyone—parents, kids, and teachers. It shows them the real-life purpose behind the things that are taught in school."

Useful Words and Expressions

introduction
  subjects
  necessary
  practical

paragraph 1
  effort
  being made
  increasingly difficult
  getting hired
  involved in
  career education
  acting out
  skills
  method
  much of
  included in
  normal classes

paragraph 2
  vocational
  back to basics
  observes
  useful
  no point

paragraph 3
  urgency
  unemployed

  jobs
  unfilled
  write a job application
  satisfactorily

paragraph 4
  projects
  going on
  workers
  explaining
  employers
  up-to-date
  information
  job opportunities

paragraph 5
  make use of
  interests
  taking trips
  interested in
  operating stores

paragraph 6
  specialists
  teachers
  business people
  local leaders
  popular
  purpose

· · · · · ·E·X·E·R·C·I·S·E·S· · · · ·

I READING COMPREHENSION

1. What is the main idea of the article?
    a. There is a great deal of unemployment in America today.
    b. There is a new emphasis on career education in American schools.
    c. Students do not need to learn Latin today.

2. Youngsters today
    a. have a more difficult time getting jobs than youngsters in the past
    b. have an easier time getting jobs than youngsters in the past
    c. are not learning practical skills

3. Training for a particular job is provided by
   a. general school studies
   b. vocational education
   c. career education

4. Career education is necessary for all of the following reasons except
   a. 19 percent of teenagers are unemployed
   b. many seventeen-year-olds cannot write a job application satisfactorily
   c. there are no available jobs

5. Career education programs include all of the following except
   a. schools are receiving information on job opportunities
   b. students are being allowed to work full time
   c. workers are telling students about their fields

6. The mechanic in paragraph 5
   a. had to hire a bookkeeper
   b. decided to become a bookkeeper
   c. went back to school to learn mathematics

7. Teachers, business people, and local leaders
   a. oppose career education
   b. do not agree on the importance of career education
   c. are working with career-education specialists

8. Mr. Hoyt believes all of the following except
   a. back to basics courses are important
   b. this approach is not popular with parents
   c. career education is important

II VOCABULARY

From the list of words below, choose the correct word for each blank space. Use each word only once.

satisfactorily	unfilled	information
skills	effort	purpose
included	increasingly	method
explaining	observes	normal

1. Educators are faced with a generation of youngsters who have an _____ difficult time getting hired.
2. Young people are taught _____ from simple bookkeeping to taking job interviews.
3. The _____ is midway between general school studies and vocational education.

4. Much of the career education is included in _____ classes that are taken by students starting with elementary school.

5. Mr. Hoyt _____, "What we're trying to do is show students how the three R's are useful".

6. Nineteen percent of teenagers are unemployed at a time when more than a million jobs are _____.

7. More than half of a group of seventeen-year-olds were unable to write a job application _____.

8. Thousands of workers are going into schools, _____ what they do and how students can get into their fields.

9. Employers are giving schools up-to-date _____ on job opportunities.

10. This way of teaching shows kids the real-life _____ behind the things they are learning at school.

III   PREPOSITIONS

Fill in the correct preposition for each blank space.

1. Faced _____ a generation _____ youngsters who have a hard time getting hired, educators are testing new methods _____ preparing students _____ employment.

2. Involved _____ what is known _____ career education is a wide variety _____ courses designed to show students how to satisfy an employer.

3. The method is midway _____ general school studies and vocational education, which provides training _____ a particular job.

4. Much _____ the career education is included _____ normal classes that are taken _____ students starting _____ elementary school.

5. Showing the urgency _____ the situation was a report that 19 percent _____ teenagers are unemployed _____ a time when more than a million jobs are unfilled.

6. Employers are giving schools up-to-date information _____ job opportunities to help young people prepare _____ careers.

7. Classes _____ Arkansas _____ New York practice economics _____ operating small stores and banks _____ school.

8. These and other projects are being organized _____ career-education specialists _____ 9,200 _____ the nation's 16,700 school districts—often _____ help _____ teachers, business people, and local leaders.

IV   COMMON EXPRESSIONS

Choose the correct expression for each blank space.

back-to-basics	acting out	going on
getting hired	no point	interested in
being made	up-to-date	much of
make use of	involved in	taking trips

1. Faced with youngsters who have a difficult time _____, educators are testing new methods of preparing students for employment.
2. _____ what is known as career education is a wide variety of courses designed to show students how to find work.
3. On-the-job visits and _____ work situations are used to teach young people skills.
4. _____ the career education is included in normal classes.
5. Vocational and _____ courses are also growing rapidly.
6. This approach is interesting a lot of kids who used to see _____ in school.
7. Among the most important projects _____ in career education, thousands of workers are going into schools, explaining how students can get into their fields.
8. Employers are giving schools _____ information on job opportunities.
9. Some projects are planned to _____ the real-life interests of young people.
10. Children _____ machines are visited by a motorcyle mechanic.

V   DEFINITE/INDEFINITE ARTICLES

Use *a/an* or *the* where needed. If no article is needed, write an X in the blank space.

To plan for _____ increased effort, 6,000 educators, business executives, and labor leaders met in _____ Houston to discuss _____ future changes in _____ career education. Showing _____ urgency of _____ situation was _____ report that 19 percent of _____ teenagers are unemployed at _____ time when more than _____ million jobs are unfilled. Another finding at _____ conference: more than half of _____ group of seventeen-year-olds studied were unable to write _____ job application satisfactorily.

VI   WORD FORMS

| | | adjectives and | |
verbs	nouns	participles	adverbs
A. increase	increase	increasing	increasingly
B. prepare	preparation	prepared	
		unprepared	
C. vary	variety	various	
D. study	studies	studious	studiously
	student		
E. use	use	useful	
		useless	

verbs	nouns	adjectives and participles	adverbs
F. inform	information	informative	informatively
G. qualify	qualifications	qualified	
		unqualified	
H. organize	organization	organized	
		disorganized	

Use the correct word in the sentences below.

A. increase, increase, increasing, increasingly
   1. The crime rate in New York _____ every year.
   2. New Yorkers are _____ worried about this.
   3. They hope to stop the _____ in crimes.
   4. Despite the _____ number of crimes, people still move to New York.

B. prepare, preparation, prepared, unprepared
   1. I wasn't _____ for the test.
   2. I wanted to _____, but I didn't have enough time.
   3. I hate to be _____ for tests.
   4. I will spend more time on _____ next time.

C. vary, variety, various
   1. This store has a great _____ of clothes.
   2. You can find anything you want in its _____ departments.
   3. The selection of clothes _____ from month to month.

D. study, studies, student, studious, studiously
   1. John has always been a good _____.
   2. He is very serious about his _____.
   3. Everyone in his family is very _____.
   4. He worked _____ in all his courses last semester.
   5. He _____ almost every night.

E. use, use, useful, useless
   1. This bicycle is broken; it is completely _____.
   2. Maybe I can get it fixed and _____ it this summer.
   3. The _____ of bicycles is common in Europe.
   4. The bicycle is a _____ invention.

F. inform, information, informative, informatively
   1. Dr. Jones spoke _____ last night.
   2. His speech was quite _____.
   3. The _____ in the speech will be very helpful.
   4. We were _____ that coffee would be served after the speech.

G. qualify, qualification, qualified, unqualified
   1. John is well _____ for this job.
   2. His _____ are quite impressive.

3. No one could say that he is _____.
4. You must have a college degree to _____ for this job.
H. organize, organization, organized, disorganized.
    1. Mr. Brown is unhappy with his secretary because she is very _____.
    2. She isn't able to _____ his papers.
    3. His last secretary used to write well _____ reports.
    4. He was always happy with her _____ of ideas.

VII   VALUES DISCUSSION

Answer the following questions, then discuss your answers with your classmates.

1. How do you feel about career education?
    a. It is good.
    b. It is not good.
    c. It is not necessary.
    d. other

2. What is the best type of career education?
    a. visiting jobs
    b. acting out working situations in class
    c. having workers come in to speak about jobs
    d. other

3. How do you feel about general school studies (subjects like history or literature, for example, that are not directly related to choosing a career)?
    a. They are good.
    b. They are not good.
    c. They are unnecessary.
    d. other

4. What school subject is the most important one?
    a. history
    b. science
    c. reading and writing
    d. other

5. What school subject is the least important?
    a. art
    b. music
    c. foreign languages
    d. other

6. How much help have you received in school in deciding on a career?
    a. no help
    b. a lot of help
    c. not enough help
    d. other

7. How good has your own education been?
   a. very good
   b. not good
   c. pretty good
   d. other

8. How is education today compared to what it was in the past?
   a. It is better.
   b. It is worse.
   c. In some ways, it is better.
   d. other

9. What is the best job to have?
   a. doctor
   b. lawyer
   c. teacher
   d. other

10. What is the best reason to choose a particular career?
    a. You can make a lot of money.
    b. Your parents want you to choose it.
    c. Everyone will respect you.
    d. other

VIII ROLEPLAYING

Choose one of the following situations to act out.

1. A career education specialist is explaining to a group of school principals and parents the importance of career education. The audience (which can be the whole class) will ask questions after a short (5 minute) talk.
2. A teacher who believes in career education is arguing with one who does not.
3. A student is telling a teacher or a school principal what he or she doesn't like about school.
4. A teacher who thinks the education system in his or her school is good is arguing with one who thinks it is bad.
5. A person who has a particular job (doctor, lawyer, policeman, fireman, for example) is telling a class of students (which can be the whole class) about his or her work. The students will then ask questions.
6. A student is talking to a counselor about what kind of work he or she wants to do in the future. (The student is not sure.)
7. An employer is interviewing someone for a particular job (decide what kind of job—a computer programmer, salesperson, mechanic, secretary) and asks about the person's education, interests, reasons for wanting the job, and so on.
8. A group of students is acting out a job situation in class (pretending to be in a bank, a small clothing store, a pet store, for example).

9. A person from your native country is talking with a person from the United States about whose education system is better.

IX   FOR DISCUSSION AND COMPOSITION

Choose one of the following to discuss or write about.

1. What is career education?
2. Why is career education being introduced into schools?
3. Did you have any kind of career education in school? If so, describe it.
4. Should schools offer career education? Why?
5. What are the advantages of "general school studies" (subjects like history or literature, for example) that are not directly related to choosing a career?
6. Are the subjects that you have studied in school practical and useful? Discuss.
7. If you could change your education, how would you like it to have been different?
8. What is wrong with education today (in the United States or in your native country)?
9. What is good about education today?
10. What job would you like to have in the future? Why?
11. If you are working, do you like your job? Why?
12. If you could have any job you wanted, what kind of work would you do? Why?

CHILDLESS—AND FREE

In the past, young married couples often had children right after getting married. They didn't ask themselves if they had the desire to stay up at night with babies, to spend a good part of their time with children, to give up° going out at night whenever they wanted to. Now,
v *many young couples feel that not having children will allow them to have a freer, more enjoyable life style.*

give...stop

1. Never has the question of family size attracted as much attention in this country as it is getting now. In this time of "the pill,"° women's liberation, and high prices, young couples are giving serious thought to the number of children they want, can afford, or can raise
5 successfully. What are the emotional or financial problems of raising a big family? Does raising children become incompatible° with a wife's working career in the outside world? Can a childless couple achieve lasting satisfaction on their own?

small ball of medicine, taken to prevent pregnancy

unable to exist with

2. Michael Shandrik, 29, and his wife Pamela, 31, have joined the
10 growing number of young couples who don't have, and don't want children. Many of their close friends are childless and plan to remain that way. Michael, a United States citizen who works for the Canadian consulate in San Francisco, says the decision not to have children developed over four years of marriage. He explains, "We never decided
15 to become childless. It more or less became an understanding after we got married." Pamela, publications editor for a travel business in Berkeley, adds, "If I had married before 23, I probably would have had

Adapted from *U.S. News & World Report* (October 4, 1976).

children. But as the years went by, I got used to the idea of working and not having children. It's too late to change now."

20 **3.**   For both of them, the desire for a free life style played a big part in the decision. Michael, who wants to build a career in communications,° makes the point honestly: "We are just too selfish to have children at this point. We would rather buy the things we really want than go without things for the sake of° the children. If we had a kid, we would
25 have to start thinking about its education and health. We like the independence of getting up and going somewhere whenever we want. I want to get ahead. I have to take a lot of risks.° In the places where I've worked, a guy who isn't happy keeps the job because of his family. I can find another job or simply leave."

T.V. and radio work

for. . .for the good of

chance of having trouble

30 **4.**   Pamela, too, is concerned about her career. But she also speaks about the need to prevent overpopulation. She says she is a supporter of Zero Population Growth,° and adds, "I am doing my part to keep the world from being overcrowded with human beings in another 100 years. Furthermore, from a woman's point of view, if you have children
35 when you are young, there is a 50-50 chance you will be raising them alone. I know a lot of divorced women with children. It's hard for them to raise their children alone."

Zero. . .the idea of stopping population growth

5.   Thus the decision has been made to remain childless. For other couples unsure of whether or not to have children, Pamela says, "If you
40 want children, it should be a positive° decision. A couple should really want to have a child and be interested in its growth. The mother should stay at home with the kid—not working and leaving it off at a day care center. A lot of women have a kid because it is what they are expected to do. Have it because you want it."

well planned

Useful Words and Expressions

introduction
  married couples
  had children
  getting married
  stay up
  spend time
  give up
paragraph 1
  family size
  attention
  the pill
  serious thought
  raise successfully

financial problems
raising children
incompatible
career
paragraph 2
joined
childless
that way
more or less
understanding
years went by
got used to

paragraph 3
  life style
  selfish
  would rather
  go without
  independence
  get ahead
paragraph 4
  prevent overpopulation
  keep the world from
    being overcrowded

furthermore
point of view
a 50-50 chance
alone
paragraph 5
  decision
  remain childless
  be interested
  stay at home
  day care center

• • • • •E•X•E•R•C•I•S•E•S• • • • •

I READING COMPREHENSION

1. What is the main idea of the article?
   a. Many young couples in the United States do not want to have children.
   b. A lot of people are thinking about family size now.
   c. The pill allows women not to have children.

2. All the following are reasons not to have children except
   a. women's liberation
   b. high prices
   c. large families

3. Michael Shandrik
   a. didn't want to have children when he got married
   b. realized he didn't want children after he got married
   c. wants to have children later

4. Pamela Shandrik
   a. feels it is too late to change now
   b. might want to have children in the future
   c. wanted to have children before she was 23

5. The Shandriks don't want to have children for all the following reasons except:
   a. They want a free life style.
   b. They like to buy what they want.
   c. They are interested in children's education.

6. In Michael's career
   a. Men with families keep a job even if they don't like it.

   b. Men with families take risks.

   c. He isn't free to change jobs.

7. Pamela feels having a child is not good
    a. if a couple is interested in its growth
    b. if the mother goes to work
    c. if the mother stays at home

8. Put the following statements in the correct order.
    a. But as the years went by, I got used to the idea of working and not having children.
    b. Pamela explains, "If I had married before 23, I probably would have had children.
    c. It's too late to change now."

II VOCABULARY

From the list of words below, choose the correct word for each blank space. Use each word only once.

selfish	serious	independence
attention	understanding	financial
joined	alone	prevent
furthermore	successfully	incompatible

1. Never has the question of family size attracted as much _____ in this country as it is getting now.
2. Young couples are giving serious thought to the number of children they want, can afford, or can raise _____.
3. What are the emotional or _____ problems of raising a big family?
4. Does raising children become _____ with a wife's working career?
5. Michael Shandrik and his wife Pamela have _____ the growing number of young couples who don't have, and don't want, children.
6. "We never decided to become childless. It more or less became an _____ after we got married."
7. "We are just too _____ to have children at this point."
8. "We like the _____ of getting up and going somewhere whenever we want."
9. "_____, from a woman's point of view, if you have children when you are young, there is a 50-50 chance you will be raising them _____."

III PREPOSITIONS

Fill in the correct preposition for each blank space.

1. Never has the question _____ family size attracted _____ much attention _____ this country _____ it is getting now.

2. _____ this time _____ "the pill," women's liberation, and high prices, young couples are giving serious thought _____ the number _____ children they want.

3. Michael, who works _____ the Canadian consulate _____ San Francisco, says the decision not to have children developed _____ four years _____ marriage.

4. _____ both _____ them, the desire _____ a free life style played a big part _____ the decision.

5. "We like the independence _____ getting _____ and going somewhere whenever we want."

6. Pamela speaks _____ the need to prevent overpopulation.

7. She says she is a supporter _____ Zero Population Growth.

8. The mother should stay _____ home _____ the kid—not working and leaving it _____ a day care center.

IV COMMON EXPRESSIONS

Choose the correct expression for each blank space.

would rather	point of view	more or less
raising children	the pill	that way
life style	got used to	a 50-50 chance
go without	keep the world from	went by

1. In this time of _____, women's liberation, and high prices, young couples are giving serious thought to the number of children they want.

2. Does _____ become incompatible with a wife's working career?

3. Many of the Shandriks close friends are childless and plan to remain _____.

4. "As the years _____, I _____ the idea of working and not having children."

5. "We _____ buy the things we really want than _____ things for the sake of the children."

6. "I am doing my part to _____ being overcrowded."

7. "From a woman's _____, if you have children when you are young, there is _____ you will be raising them alone."

V DEFINITE/INDEFINITE ARTICLES

Use *a/an* or *the* where needed. If no article is needed, write an X in the blank space.

For _____ Shandriks, _____ desire for _____ free life style played _____ big part in _____ decision not to have children. Michael, who wants to build _____ career in _____ communications, makes _____ point honestly: "We are just too selfish to have _____ children at this point. We would rather buy _____ things we really want than go without _____ things for _____ sake of _____ children. If we had _____ kid, we would have to start thinking about its education and health. We like _____ independence of getting up and going somewhere whenever we want."

VI WORD FORMS

verbs	nouns	adjectives and participles	adverbs
A. question	question	questionable	
B. liberate	liberation	liberated	
		unliberated	
C. think	thought	thoughtful	thoughtfully
		thoughtless	thoughtlessly
D. succeed	success	successful	successfully
E. develop	development	developed	
		undeveloped	
F. communicate	communication	communicative	
		uncommunicative	
G. prevent	prevention	preventive	
H. grow	growth	growing	

Use the correct word in the sentences below.

A. question, question, questionable
   1. I don't think that chair is very good; its quality is _____.
   2. I wanted to ask Dr. Jones a few _____ after his lecture.
   3. I especially wanted to _____ him about his economic theories.
B. liberate, liberation, liberated, unliberated
   1. Jane feels that she should have the same rights as men; she is a _____ woman.
   2. _____ women accept an inferior position in society.
   3. Women's _____ has caused some problems in families.
   4. Our society must change in order for women to _____ themselves from their traditional roles.
C. think, thought, thoughtful, thoughtless, thoughtfully, thoughtlessly
   1. It was _____ of me to forget Mary's birthday.
   2. John _____ chose a very nice present for Mary's birthday, but he _____ forgot to give it to her on time.
   3. I like John because he is very _____.
   4. I have given a great deal of _____ to this problem, and I _____ I have found a solution.
D. succeed, success, successful, successfully
   1. John gets good grades in school; he is a _____ student.
   2. I'm sure he will be a _____ in his chosen career.
   3. He _____ took five classes this semester.
   4. You must work hard if you want to _____.

E. develop, development, developed, undeveloped
1. In general, countries with a lot of industries are considered _____,
   and those without industries are considered _____.
2. Many countries want to _____ more industries.
3. The _____ of its economy is one of a country's major concerns.

F. communicate, communication, communicative, uncommunicative
1. Bill doesn't talk much; he is very _____.
2. His wife wishes he were more _____.
3. There is a lack of _____ between young people and old people.
4. It is unfortunate that young and old people don't _____ more with
   each other.

G. prevent, prevention, preventive
1. An old proverb says, "An ounce of _____ is worth a pound of
   cure."
2. The idea of _____ medicine is to _____ people from
   getting sick, rather than to cure people who already are sick.

H. grow, growth, growing
1. Solar energy is a _____ industry.
2. Its _____ will increase in the next few years.
3. If it _____, people may not have to depend so much on oil for
   energy.

VII VALUES DISCUSSION

Answer the following questions. Then discuss your answers with your classmates.

1. How do you feel about having children?
   a. It is a good thing to do.
   b. It is not a good thing to do.
   c. It is good when you are older.
   d. other

2. How do you feel about the Shandriks not wanting to have children?
   a. They are very selfish.
   b. It is the best thing for them.
   c. They will be sorry when they are older.
   d. other

3. What is the greatest advantage of having children?
   a. seeing the children grow up
   b. having someone to care about you when you are older
   c. making a contribution to society
   d. other

4. What is the greatest disadvantage of having children?
   a. spending all your money on them
   b. not having any free time

      c. not getting respect and obedience
      d. other

5. What is the best age for a man to have children?
      a. 20
      b. 25
      c. 35
      d. other

6. What is the best age for a woman to have children?
      a. 20
      b. 25
      c. 35
      d. other

7. What is the best number of children to have?
      a. one
      b. two
      c. five
      d. other

8. Is it possible for a woman to work and be a good mother?
      a. yes
      b. no
      c. after a child is six years old
      d. other

9. How do you feel about day care centers (in the United States or in your native country)?
      a. They are good places.
      b. They are bad places.
      c. They could be good if the government spent more money on them.
      d. other

10. How do you feel about the way children are raised in your native country compared to the way they are raised in the United States?
      a. It is better in the United States.
      b. It is better in my native country.
      c. In my native country, it is better for the children, but worse for the women.
      d. other

11. How do you feel about "nuclear families" (a father, mother, and children living together) compared to "extended families" (which include grand-parents as well as perhaps uncles and aunts all living in the same house)?
      a. Nuclear families are better.
      b. Extended families are better.
      c. They are both the same.
      d. other

VIII   ROLEPLAYING

Choose one of the following situations to act out.

1. Michael Shandrik is explaining to a friend why he doesn't want children.
2. A friend who has children is trying to convince Michael to have children.
3. Pamela Shandrik is explaining to a friend why she doesn't want children.
4. A friend is trying to convince Pamela to have children.
5. Two people who have children are discussing the advantages and disadvantages of having children.
6. Two women who work are discussing why it is difficult for women to work and have children.
7. Michael's parents (mother and father) are trying to convince him to have children.
8. Pamela's parents are trying to convince her to have children.
9. An expert on overpopulation is telling a group (which can be the whole class) why this is a serious problem. The group can then ask questions.
10. A woman who works and leaves her child at a day care center is telling a friend why she feels it is okay to do this.
11. A person from your native country is arguing with a person from the United States about which country has a better way of raising children.
12. A person who believes nuclear families (a father, mother, and children living together) are better, is arguing with someone who feels extended families (with grandparents and perhaps uncles and aunts all living together) are better.

IX   FOR DISCUSSION AND COMPOSITION

Choose one of the following to discuss or write about.

1. Why don't the Shandriks want to have children?
2. What are the disadvantages of having children?
3. What are the advantages of having children?
4. If you don't have children, do you want to in the future? Why?
5. If you have children, tell what you like or dislike about having children.
6. Is it possible for a woman to work and be a good mother? Discuss.
7. Are day care centers good places to leave children? Why?
8. What is "overpopulation"? Why might this be a serious problem in the future?
9. Describe how children are raised in your native country.
10. Compare how children are raised in your native country and in the United States.
11. In some countries, people usually live in "nuclear families" (a father, mother, and children living together) and in other countries, people live in "extended families" (with grandparents and perhaps uncles and aunts all living in the same house). Describe the family system in your native country.
12. Which system is better: nuclear families or extended families? Why?

HEALTH

HOW TO EAT RIGHT AND LIVE LONGER

Interview with Dr. Jean Mayer, Authority on Nutrition*

In recent years, we have become more concerned about the food we eat. We hear that certain chemicals in our food can cause cancer and other serious diseases. Dr. Mayer presents a less frightening picture of modern foods than we sometimes hear in the news and also gives us ∨ *some good advice on how to stay healthy.*

Q. Dr. Mayer, we're constantly being told that a lot of things we eat are bad for us—will kill us or give us some disease. Has much of our food become dangerous to health?

A. There are a lot of exaggerations° and unnecessary fears about this.
5   The great American supermarket is a wonderful place with a much greater variety of healthy food than has ever been available before. If you know something about nutrition and about shopping, you can go into a typical supermarket and come out with an excellent diet.° You can also come out with a terrible diet if you don't know
10   anything about nutrition.

Q. How do you explain the common feeling that more disease is caused today by the food we eat than in the past?

A. I think we've learned more about the relations between food and health. Let me give you an example of what we do know. We know
15   that being overweight is bad for people. The evidence° is that being just a little overweight probably is not dangerous to health, unless some other disease is present, like diabetes or hypertension. But

saying more than the truth

sort of food eaten by someone

studies that prove something

*the study of food values

Adapted from *U.S. News & World Report* (August 9, 1976).

being very overweight is bad for health, not only because it makes
any existing disease much worse, but also because being overweight
20   makes it more likely that you will become diabetic or hypertensive.
Q. Is there a connection between diet and particular diseases? For
example, can what we eat cause cancer?
A. We suspect that diet is related to most types of cancer but we don't
have definite proof. For example, one very popular theory is that
25   cancer of the colon° is caused by the lack of fiber in our diet. It is a   lower part of the large
fact that cancer of the colon is very much more common among   intestine
people who live in industrialized countries than among people
who live in undeveloped societies. Researchers have discovered that
if you have a lot of fiber in your diet—such as the fiber in vegetables
30   and cereals—your food moves faster through your intestines. The
theory is that if the food moves quickly, it does not produce cancer-
causing substances (carcinogens), but the theory is not definitely
proven.
Q. What about stomach cancer?
35 A. On that we have some good news. Cancer of the stomach was, 30
years ago, an extremely common form of cancer. In recent years, the
number of cases of stomach cancer has decreased. One theory is that
the amount of rancidity in fats has been cut down by improved
refrigeration and the use of preservatives. It is thought that rancid°   gone bad, spoiled
40   fats may be carcinogenic. We do know that there is a very high
frequency of stomach cancer in countries which do a lot of frying
and keep on reusing the same fat all the time.
Q. Food additives also are causing a lot of concern. Do you consider
these dangerous?
45 A. First of all, the word *additive* is a very general one describing
anything that you add to food. You could argue that, in a sense,°   **in**...in a way
the most dangerous food additive is salt, and that sugar is also a
dangerous food additive. Until the recent upset about the possible
dangerous effects of the food coloring Red Dye Number 2, which
50   only made food look good and made no contribution to health or
safety, it seems to me that people were most excited about those very
additives which are most useful and least dangerous.
Q. Such as?
A. Such as preservatives, which basically stop molds.° Some of the   plant growth that
55   most common molds can cause cancer. For instance, aflatoxin is a   appears on food
strong and dangerous carcinogen produced by a common mold
which grows on peanuts, corn, milk, bread—pretty much
anywhere. We protect ourselves against it in part with preservatives.

· · ·

Q. You mentioned earlier that sugar and salt might be dangerous.
60   What do you mean by that?
A. Let's take sugar first. It is found everywhere in our diet. The
average American man, woman, or child eats 125 pounds per year.

Well, 125 pounds a year is a lot of "empty" calories,° lacking in
proteins, vitamins, and minerals. Certainly, if you're going to
65   control overweight, you should start by cutting down on sugar.
Also, it is bad for your teeth. And there is some evidence that eating
large amounts of sugar can cause diabetes and heart disease.

units of energy given by food

Q. And salt?

A. People react to° salt differently, but eating a lot of salt can cause
70   hypertension.

react...respond to

. . .

Q. Dr. Mayer, why is it that Americans have a more serious problem
with overweight than people in other countries?

A. The best evidence we have suggests that it's not because we eat so
much food. Our big problem is exercise—the fact that in 1900
75   Henry Ford started producing automobiles and since World War II
we have produced a large number of labor-saving devices both for
industry and for the home. The physical activity of men and
women has decreased since 1900.

Q. Do you mean that exercise is really the key to overweight, rather
80   than what we eat or how much we eat?

A. For most people, inactivity is the most important cause of their
slowly gaining weight over the years. In other words, most people
who have a weight problem at age 45 nowadays would not have had
a weight problem in 1630 when they would have walked
85   everywhere, cut wood, worked in their fields, and so on.

Q. If people tend to be overweight, how much exercise should they
get?

A. You have to be reasonable about this. People gain weight for 20
years and then they want to lose it in two months. You should look
90   at exercise as a way of maintaining° a good weight rather than as an
emergency way of losing weight. Let me explain it this way: a
pound of fat is equal to 3,500 calories and 100 calories is used up by
walking 20 minutes. So a 20 minute walk daily will take off 10
pounds of fat over a year. If you walk quickly, you will use abut 300
95   calories an hour. If you play tennis vigorously° you use perhaps 400
or 500. If you chopped wood for half an hour a day, you could take
off 26 pounds of fat a year. That is pretty good. Obviously,° if you
want to lose weight very quickly, you should do two things at the
same time: eat less and exercise more!

keeping

with great effort

clearly

Useful Words and Expressions

Introduction   chemicals
  concerned   cancer
  food   diseases

advice
stay healthy
questions 1 and 2
  constantly
  dangerous
  exaggerations
  variety
  available
  nutrition
  diet
  overweight
  evidence
  a little
  diabetes
  hypertension
questions 3 and 4
  cause
  cancer
  suspect
  cancer of the colon
  related
  lack of fiber
  in recent years
  stomach cancer
  decreased
  keep on
  fat
  all the time
questions 5 and 6
  additives

general
in a sense
upset
look good
preservatives
protect
in part
questions 7 and 8
  sugar
  salt
  lacking
  proteins
  vitamins
  minerals
  control overweight
  cutting down
questions 9, 10, and 11
  exercise
  automobiles
  labor-saving devices
  physical activity
  gaining weight
  in other words
  walked
  cut wood
  tend
  reasonable
  emergency
  obviously
  at the same time

• • • • •E•X•E•R•C•I•S•E•S• • • • • •

I READING COMPREHENSION

1. What is the main idea of the article?
    a. If you are careful, it is possible to have a healthy diet.
    b. Food is worse today than it used to be.
    c. Much of our food today causes cancer.

2. The American supermarket
    a. does not have healthy food

b. only has healthy food
c. has a lot of healthy food

3. What is not true about being overweight?
   a. It can cause diabetes or hypertension.
   b. It makes any existing disease worse.
   c. It is always dangerous.

4. Cancer of the colon
   a. is not related to fiber
   b. is more common in industrialized countries
   c. is more common in undeveloped societies

5. Food additives
   a. can stop molds
   b. are always dangerous
   c. make no contribution to health

6. Sugar
   a. lacks protein, vitamins, and minerals
   b. does not have many calories
   c. causes hypertension

7. People are overweight for all the following reasons except
   a. They use labor-saving devices.
   b. They don't get enough exercise.
   c. They walk everywhere.

8. Put the following statements in the correct order.
   a. We know that being overweight is bad for people.
   b. But being very overweight is bad for health.
   c. Let me give you an example of what we do know.
   d. The evidence is that being just a little overweight probably is not dangerous to health.

II VOCABULARY

From the list of words below, choose the correct word for each blank space. Use each word only once.

general	exaggerations	emergency
available	reasonable	cause
tend	upset	constantly
suspect	evidence	obviously

1. We're _____ being told that a lot of things we eat are bad for us.

2. There are a lot of _____ and unnecessary fears about this.

3. The great American supermarket is a wonderful place with a much greater variety of healthy food than has ever been _____ before.

4. The _____ is that being just a little overweight probably is not dangerous to health.

5. We _____ that diet is related to most types of cancer.

6. The word *additive* is a very _____ one.

7. Until the recent _____ about Red Dye Number 2, people were most excited about those very additives which are most useful and least dangerous.

8. If people _____ to be overweight, how much exercise should they get?

9. You should not look at exercise as an _____ way of losing weight.

10. _____, if you want to lose weight very quickly, you should do two things: eat less and exercise more!

III PREPOSITIONS

Fill in the correct preposition for each blank space.

1. The great American supermarket is a wonderful place _____ a much greater variety _____ healthy food than has ever been available before.

2. We suspect that diet is related _____ most types _____ cancer. _____ example, one very popular theory is that cancer _____ the colon is caused _____ the lack _____ fiber in our diet.

3. One theory is that the amount _____ rancidity _____ fats has been cut _____ _____ improved refrigeration and the use _____ preservatives.

4. Until the recent upset _____ Red Dye Number 2, which made no contribution _____ health, it seems _____ me that people were most excited _____ those very additives which are most useful.

5. Aflatoxin is a strong and dangerous carcinogen produced _____ a common mold which grows _____ peanuts, corn, milk, bread—pretty much anywhere.

6. Certainly, if you're going to control overweight, you should start _____ cutting down _____ sugar. Also, it is bad _____ your teeth.

7. _____ 1900 Henry Ford started producing automobiles and _____ World War II we have produced a large number _____ labor-saving devices both _____ industry and _____ the home.

8. You have to be reasonable _____ losing weight. People gain weight _____ 20 years and then they want to lose it _____ two months.

IV COMMON EXPRESSIONS

Choose the correct expression for each blank space.

a little	keep on	gaining weight
in recent years	in other words	look good
labor-saving devices	in part	at the same time
all the time	in a sense	lack of

1. _____, the number of cases of stomach cancer has decreased.
2. There is a very high frequency of stomach cancer in countries which do a lot of frying and which keep reusing the same fat _____.
3. You could argue that, _____, the most dangerous food additive is salt.
4. Until the recent upset about Red Dye Number 2, which only made food _____, people were most excited about those very additives which are most useful.
5. We protect ourselves against aflatoxin _____ with preservatives.
6. Since World War II we have produced a large number of _____ both for industry and for the home.
7. For most people, inactivity is the most important cause of their slowly _____ over the years. _____, most people who have a weight problem at age 45 nowadays would not have had a weight problem in 1630.
8. Obviously, if you want to lose weight very quickly, you should do two things _____: eat less and exercise more!

V   DEFINITE/INDEFINITE ARTICLES

Use *a/an* or *the* where needed. If no article is needed, write an X in the blank spaces.

Q. Is there _____ connection between _____ diet and _____ particular diseases? For example, can what we eat cause _____ cancer?

A. We suspect that _____ diet is related to _____ most types of _____ cancer but we don't have _____ definite proof. For example, one very popular theory is that _____ cancer of _____ colon is caused by _____ lack of _____ fiber in our diet. It is _____ fact that _____ cancer of _____ colon is very much more common among _____ people who live in _____ industrialized countries than among _____ people who live in _____ undeveloped societies. _____ researchers have discovered that if you have a lot of _____ fiber in your diet—such as _____ fiber in _____ vegetables and _____ cereals—your food moves faster through your intestines. _____ theory is that if _____ food moves quickly, it does not produce _____ cancer-causing substances, but _____ theory is not definitely proven.

VI   WORD FORMS

verbs	nouns	adjectives and participles	adverbs
A. endanger	danger	dangerous	dangerously
B. relate	relation	related	relatively
	relationship	unrelated	
C. suspect	suspicion	suspicious	suspiciously
D.	frequency	frequent	frequently
		infrequent	infrequently

verbs	nouns	adjectives and participles	adverbs
E. argue	argument	argumentative	
F.	possibility	possible	possibly
		impossible	
G. excite	excitement	excited	
		exciting	
H. reason	reason	reasonable	reasonably
		unreasonable	

Use the correct word in the sentences below.

A. endanger, danger, dangerous, dangerously
   1. The life of a fireman is _____.
   2. He lives _____.
   3. You will _____ your life if you drive in such a heavy rain.
   4. There is a _____ that you may have an accident.

B. relate, relation, relationship, related, unrelated, relatively
   1. I don't understand why you said that; it is not _____ to this discussion.
   2. Please don't make any more _____ comments.
   3. The _____ between diet and health is clear.
   4. Margarine is a _____ good food.
   5. George doesn't have a very good _____ with his parents.
   6. He _____ to his friends much better.

C. suspect, suspicion, suspicious, suspiciously
   1. Be careful! A _____ looking man is following you.
   2. He is looking at you _____.
   3. I _____ that you may be in danger.
   4. I hope my _____ is incorrect.

D. frequency, frequent, infrequent, frequently, infrequently
   1. Jane visits her parents _____.
   2. They appreciate her _____ visits.
   3. On the other hand, her brother George only comes _____.
   4. They wish his visits weren't so _____.
   5. The _____ of Jane's visits shows her concern for her parents.

E. argue, argument, argumentative
   1. I just had a big _____ with Bob.
   2. He always _____ with everybody.
   3. He shouldn't be so _____.

F. possibility, possible, impossible, possibly
   1. I'm sorry, it is not _____ for me to help you now.
   2. _____, I can help you tomorrow.
   3. Even tomorrow, if I don't finish my work, it will be _____ for me to help you.
   4. There is a _____ that John might be able to help you.

G. excite, excitement, excited, exciting
  1. Everyone was very _____ at the concert.
  2. I haven't seen so much _____ in a long time.
  3. Not all performers have the ability to _____ an audience like that.
  4. The newspapers said it was an _____ performance.
H. reason, reason, reasonable, unreasonable, unreasonably
  1. I don't understand why Sam is mad at Jane; I think he is being _____.
  2. Usually, he is a very _____ person.
  3. I tried to speak to him _____, but he could give me no _____ why he was angry.
  4. Maybe you should try to _____ with him about it.

VII VALUES DISCUSSION

Answer the following questions. Then discuss your answers with your classmates.

  1. How do you feel about the foods we eat today?
    a. They are good.
    b. They are bad.
    c. They are worse than in the past.
    d. other

  2. How do you feel about your own diet?
    a. It is good.
    b. It is bad.
    c. It is good enough.
    d. other

  3. What is the worst of the following health problems?
    a. diabetes
    b. hypertension
    c. heart trouble
    d. overweight

  4. What is the best thing you could do about your diet?
    a. Eat less.
    b. Eat more.
    c. Eat more vegetables.
    d. other

  5. What is the best thing you could do about your health?
    a. Sleep more.
    b. Get more exercise.
    c. Move to a different place.
    d. other

  6. How do you feel about preservatives?
    a. They are good.

b. They are bad.
c. They are necessary.
d. other

7. How is the diet of people in your native country?
   a. good
   b. bad
   c. good for a few
   d. other

8. How is the diet of people in your native country compared to that of people in the United States?
   a. better
   b. worse
   c. the same
   d. other

9. How do you feel about exercise?
   a. I like it.
   b. I don't like it.
   c. I like some kinds.
   d. other

10. How do you feel about the amount of exercise you get?
    a. I should get more.
    b. I get enough.
    c. I get too much.
    d. other

11. How do you feel about someone being overweight?
    a. It is a terrible problem.
    b. It is not a serious problem.
    c. It is a good thing.
    d. other

12. How do you feel about cars?
    a. They are good.
    b. They are bad.
    c. They are not necessary.
    d. other

VIII   ROLEPLAYING

Choose one of the following situations to act out.

1. An audience (which can be the whole class) is asking Dr. Mayer questions about nutrition (for example, about a healthy diet, diet and disease, cancer, preservatives, exercise).

2. A housewife who knows a lot about nutrition is giving advice to one who knows nothing about it.

3. A reporter is interviewing Dr. Mayer on one of the subjects mentioned in the text.

4. A mother is explaining to a child why he or she should eat certain healthy foods.

5. A doctor is giving advice to a person with a health problem (diabetes, hypertension, heart trouble, overweight, for example).

6. A person from your native country is talking with a person from the United States about who has a healthier diet.

7. An American is explaining to a reporter why he or she doesn't get more exercise (mentioning the car and other kinds of labor-saving devices).

8. Two Americans are talking about how much exercise they get and if they could get more.

9. An overweight person is talking with a friend about the need to lose weight and how to do it.

10. Two people (one who has a car and one who doesn't) are talking about the advantages and disadvantages of having a car.

IX FOR DISCUSSION AND COMPOSITION

Choose one of the following to discuss or write about.

1. Are the foods that we eat today healthy? Discuss.

2. Is your own diet healthy? How could you make it healthier?

3. In what ways could you improve your health? Discuss not only diet but also exercise, sleep, work, and so on.

4. Discuss some common health problems that people have today, their causes, and how to solve them.

5. What do we know about cancer today? Do you think a cure for cancer will be found soon? Why?

6. Describe the typical diet of people in your native country. Is it healthy? Why?

7. Compare the diets of people in your native country and in the United States. Which is healthier? Why?

8. Why don't Americans get enough exercise? Discuss a few specific causes.

9. Describe the types and amount of exercise that people in your native country usually get. Do they get enough? Why?

10. Describe the type and amount of exercise that you usually get. Do you get enough? Why?

11. If you were overweight, what would you do?

12. Do you know anyone who is overweight? If so, explain why that person is overweight. What could he or she do about it? Do you think the person will take off weight in the future? Why?

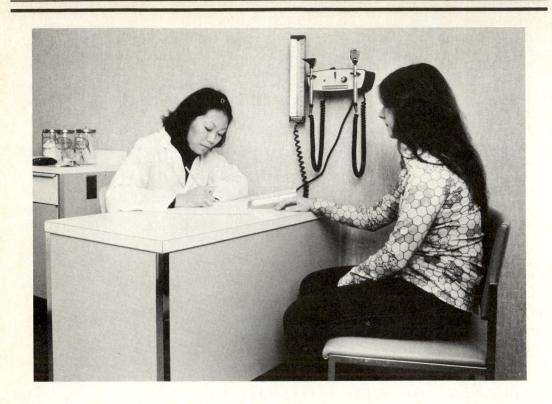

HEALTH CARE: CAN THE UNITED STATES LEARN FROM OTHER COUNTRIES?

Americans spend a lot of money on health care. It has been suggested that we might spend less money and get better health care if we developed a national health program, such as the ones that exist in Britain, Sweden, or the Soviet Union. Such a national health program
v *though, could also have disadvantages, including high taxes and a less personal doctor-patient relationship.*

1. Joe Gannon, the young doctor of the T.V. program Medical Center, is too nice a guy to mention it. Anyone watching this program from a hospital bed, however, knows what is missing from those weekly T.V. medical adventures. Getting sick costs money—lots of
5 money.

2. Even though Gannon doesn't pay much attention to it, the cost of health care in the United States has become a serious problem. Americans spend more money on health care than people of any other nation. Last year the bill was $118 billion, up 14 percent from 1974. To
10 put it on a more personal level, that's $550 a year for every man, woman, and child in the country. Before long, it is expected to be more than $600.

3. Why does health care cost so much? One reason is the high cost of new drugs and medical equipment, including computers. Much of the
15 cost, however, may be due to our way of paying the bills. "The doctor

who orders hospitalization or drugs has no reason to be economical,° | **be**...try to save money
since he doesn't pay for them,'' reports *Science Digest*. ''The patient
doesn't have any control over what is being ordered. The bill, or at least
a large part of it, in the case of someone who is insured, goes to the
20 insurance company.° The company simply pays without having any | **insurance**...company that takes payments to guard against loss or sickness
say in what is being ordered. The system tends to produce
overspending.'' Of course, not everyone just sits back and has the bills
paid by an insurance company. Not all Americans have insurance, or
enough insurance. A serious illness, or a lot of little ones, can use up
25 the family savings.° | money that is saved

4.   But even with all the money being spent, the United States does not
have the world's best health care. Eighteen countries have lower rates of
infant deaths and a longer life expectancy.° Most Americans say the | **life**...normal length of life
United States should follow some other countries and set up required
30 government health insurance. They argue:
—Proper health care is a right that all people—rich or poor—must get.
As it is now, only the rich can afford it, and the middle-income family
can be ruined trying to pay for it.
—The quality and cost of such a program could be controlled by
35 government rules.

5.   On the other hand, opponents—many of them doctors—say:
—Costs would increase greatly and medical treatment would become
worse because people would be encouraged to visit a doctor for every
little ache and pain.
40 —A big government-controlled program would destroy the personal
relationship between doctor and patient, and would make health care
less efficient.° | able to produce the desired result quickly

6.   Health care in other countries goes from terrible to excellent. Many
of the poorest nations spend less than one dollar a year per citizen for
45 health care, says the World Health Organization, a United Nations
agency. These, of course, are not the countries Americans look at when
they discuss the advantages of national health insurance. Three
countries in particular—Britain, Sweden, and the Soviet Union—have
been studied by Americans who want a better system of health care:
50 *Britain*: Compulsory° insurance covers all citizens. Patients can have | required
their own doctor. Drugs, hospitalization, and treatment all are free. A
private hospital bed is available at $2 to $5 a day. The program is 90
percent financed from general tax income, the rest by small
contributions from workers and employers.
55 *Sweden*: Compulsory. Each county is required to provide health care
for residents;° 70 percent to 80 percent of the counties' yearly expense | people who live there
goes to health care, financed by a county income tax of 10 percent. The
patient pays about $3.75 for each clinic° visit, $2.50 per day for in- | part of a hospital
hospital care. There is a full-time doctor at all companies with 1,000 or

60 more employees. Workers receive 90 percent of their salary° during
    sickness.

    The Soviet Union: All medical treatment is free, including drugs and
    medicine. Expectant mothers receive payments for ten weeks before and
    after childbirth. Workers receive sick pay during illness. Employees

65 who work in unhealthy or very difficult conditions may be able to
    retire from work° five to ten years early. All doctors are government
    employees, their salaries controlled by the government.

7. "Free" anything sounds good. But, of course, nothing is really free.
    The people do pay through taxes. And even in countries where

70 "socialized medicine" has been practiced for a long time, not everyone
    is entirely pleased. "Oh, it's a great system if you are sick," a Swedish
    business executive said. "But otherwise you just end up paying too
    much in taxes, up to 80 percent of your salary if you are highly paid."
    A British government study earlier this year showed National Health

75 Service lacked money, equipment, and medical staff.° That means
    non-emergency cases often have to wait. "The treatment is good once
    you get into the hospital," said one Englishman. "It's the getting in
    that's the problem." Information is hard to get from totalitarian
    countries, but there doesn't seem to be much of a "doctor-patient"

80 relationship in the Soviet Union. This past summer the Communist
    Party Congress recommended a kind of assembly-line° medicine in
    huge clinics around the country. The goal is to save time and money.

8. Are the problems caused by a system of national health care greater
    than the benefits?° Is the cost of providing satisfactory health care for

85 all worth it? Or does the answer lie somewhere between private health
    care and national health care? These are questions we will be hearing
    about for a long time to come.

money that you earn on a job

retire...stop working

medical...doctors, nurses, and so on

kind of mass production, with a product moving by a line of people

advantages

Useful Words and Expressions

introduction
  health care
  national health program
  disadvantages
  high taxes
  doctor-patient relationship
paragraph 1
  missing
  medical adventures
  getting sick
  money
paragraph 2
  pay attention to
  cost

a serious problem
before long
expected
paragraph 3
  drugs
  medical equipment
  due to
  way of paying
  doctor
  has no reason
  economical
  the insurance company
  having any say
  has the bills paid

use up
the family savings
paragraph 4
set up
required
government health insurance
the rich
afford
paragraph 5
opponents
costs
increase
visit
destroy
personal relationship
efficient

paragraph 6
a better system
compulsory insurance
tax income
county
residents
sick pay
paragraph 7
free
sounds good
taxes
otherwise
salary
paragraph 8
problems
benefits
hearing about

• • • • •E•X•E•R•C•I•S•E•S• • • • • •

I READING COMPREHENSION

1. What is the main idea of the article?
    a. It might be good for the United States to have a system of national health care.
    b. Medical bills are very high in the United States.
    c. Doctors are opposed to national health care.

2. What does Joe Gannon not mention?
    a. getting sick
    b. medical adventures
    c. money

3. Health care is expensive because of all the following except
    a. New drugs are expensive.
    b. The patient controls what is ordered.
    c. The doctor has no reason to be economical.

4. The United States should set up required government health insurance for all of the following reasons except
    a. Proper health care is a right.

b. Middle-income families can be ruined by medical expenses.

c. Costs would increase greatly.

5. Which of the following is not true in Britain?

   a. The program is completely financed from tax income.

   b. Patients can have their own doctor.

   c. Drugs, hospitalization, and treatment are free.

6. A Swedish business executive says

   a. The system keeps you from getting sick.

   b. The system is good for people with a lot of money.

   c. The system costs too much money.

7. In Russia

   a. The doctors are private employees.

   b. The government wants to save time and money.

   c. There is a good doctor-patient relationship.

8. According to the author

   a. We will be hearing about national health care for a long time.

   b. National health care causes too many problems.

   c. National health care is too expensive.

II VOCABULARY

From the list of words below, choose the correct word for each blank space. Use each word only once.

economical	required	opponents
destroy	efficient	afford
otherwise	expected	benefits
equipment	missing	visit

1. Anyone who is watching this program from a hospital bed knows what is _____ from those weekly T.V. medical adventures.

2. Why does health care cost so much? One reason is the high cost of new drugs and medical _____

3. "The doctor who orders hospitalization or drugs has no reason to be _____."

4. Many Americans say the United States should set up _____ government health insurance.

5. As it is now, only the rich can _____ proper health care.

6. _____—many of them doctors—say costs would increase greatly.

7. People would be encouraged to _____ a doctor for every little ache and pain.

8. A big government-controlled program would make health care less _____.

9. "It's a great system if you are sick, but _____ you just end up paying too much in taxes."

10. Are the problems caused by a system of national health care greater than the _____?

III PREPOSITIONS

Fill in the correct preposition for each blank space.

1. Even though Gannon doesn't pay much attention _____ it, the cost _____ health care _____ the United States has become a serious problem.

2. The bill, or _____ least a large part _____ it, _____ the case _____ someone who is insured, goes _____ the insurance company.

3. The quality and cost _____ a government health insurance program could be controlled _____ government rules.

4. Health care _____ other countries goes _____ terrible _____ excellent.

5. Many _____ the poorest nations spend less than one dollar a year per citizen _____ health care.

6. _____ Sweden 70 percent _____ 80 percent _____ the counties' yearly expense goes _____ health care.

7. Even _____ countries where socialized medicine has been practiced _____ a long time, not everyone is entirely pleased.

8. Are the problems caused _____ a system _____ national health care greater than the benefits?

IV COMMON EXPRESSIONS

Choose the correct expression for each blank space.

pay attention to	has no reason	set up
use up	hearing about	has the bills paid
personal relationship	before long	sounds good
getting sick	having any say	due to

1. _____ costs money—lots of money.

2. Even though Gannon doesn't _____ it, the cost of health care in the United States has become a serious problem.

3. _____ it is expected to be more than $600 a year per person.

4. Much of the cost may be _____ our way of paying the bills.

5. The insurance company pays without _____ in what is being ordered.

6. Not everyone just sits back and _____ by an insurance company.

7. A serious illness can _____ the family savings.

8. A big government-controlled program would destroy the _____ between doctor and patient.

9. "Free" anything _____.
10. These are questions we will be _____ for some time.

V DEFINITE/INDEFINITE ARTICLES

Use *a/an* or *the* where needed. If no article is needed, write an X in the blank space.

Even though Gannon doesn't pay much attention to it, _____ cost of _____ health care in _____ United States has become _____ serious problem. _____ Americans spend more money on _____ health care than _____ people of _____ any other nation. _____ last year _____ bill was $118 billion, up 14 percent from 1974. To put it on _____ more personal level, that's $550 _____ year for every man, woman, and child in _____ country. Before long, it is expected to be more than $600.

VI WORD FORMS

	verbs	nouns	adjectives and participles	adverbs
A.		medicine	medical	medically
B.		adventure	adventurous	adventurously
C.		person	personal	personally
D.	hospitalize	hospital	hospitalized	
		hospitalization		
E.	require	requirement	required	
F.	oppose	opposition	opposed	
		opponent		
G.		efficiency	efficient	efficiently
H.	please	pleasure	pleasant	pleasantly
			unpleasant	
			pleased	

Use the correct word in the sentences below.

A. medicine, medical, medically
   1. I appreciated Dr. Brown's _____ advice.
   2. I think his advice was _____ correct.
   3. He doesn't think I need to take any _____.
B. adventure, adventurous, adventurously
   1. Tom lives _____.
   2. He is an _____ young man.
   3. He likes to tell stories about his _____.
C. person, personal, personally
   1. _____, I don't think you should go to Sarah's party.

2. She really isn't a very nice _____.

3. Of course, that's only my _____ opinion.

D. hospitalize, hospital, hospitalization, hospitalized

   1. They had to _____ John last week.

   2. His _____ upset his family a great deal.

   3. The _____ where he is staying is nice but we hope he won't have to be _____ too long.

E. require, requirement, required

   1. Chemistry is a _____ subject in this school.

   2. They also _____ that you take philosophy and sociology.

   3. I wish they didn't have so many _____.

F. oppose, opposition, opponent, opposed

   1. George encountered strong _____ to his plan.

   2. He didn't think so many people would _____ it.

   3. Sam, his major _____, has always been _____ to plans of that sort.

G. efficiency, efficient, efficiently

   1. Mr. Smith's secretary is very _____.

   2. He does all Mr. Smith's work _____.

   3. The _____ of the office has improved since he started working here.

H. please, pleasure, pleasant, unpleasant, pleased, pleasantly

   1. It was a great _____ to see you at the party last night.

   2. The party was _____, but the loud music was rather _____.

   3. I am _____ that my children behaved so _____ last night.

   4. Could you _____ call me tonight?

VII VALUES DISCUSSION

Answer the following questions. Then discuss your answers with your classmates.

  1. What is the best thing about private health care?
    a. There is a good doctor-patient relationship.
    b. The doctors are well qualified.
    c. People only go to see a doctor when it's necessary.
    d. other

  2. What is the best thing about national health care?
    a. The government can control the prices.
    b. The government can control the quality.
    c. People will go to doctors more often.
    d. other

  3. How do you feel about private compared to national health care?
    a. Private health care is better.

    b. National health care is better.
    c. They are both bad.
    d. other

4. What do you think of the health care system in the United States?
    a. It is good.
    b. It is bad.
    c. It is better than in most other countries.
    d. other

5. What do you think of the health care system in your native country?
    a. It is good.
    b. It is bad.
    c. It is better than in the United States.
    d. other

6. What is the most important thing about health care?
    a. It should be inexpensive.
    b. The doctors should be well qualified.
    c. There should be a good doctor-patient relationship.
    d. other

7. If you were a doctor, where would you like to work?
    a. in the United States
    b. in Britain
    c. in my native country
    d. other

8. How do you feel about most doctors?
    a. They are good.
    b. They are bad.
    c. They don't know much.
    d. other

9. How do you feel about hospitals?
    a. They are wonderful places.
    b. They are terrible places.
    c. I am afraid of them.
    d. other

10. How do you feel about the health care you have received in your life?
    a. It has been good.
    b. It has been bad.
    c. I don't know if it has been good or bad.
    d. other

VIII ROLEPLAYING

Choose one of the following situations to act out.

1. A doctor is telling a reporter why private health care is better than national health care.
2. A middle-income person in the United States is complaining to a reporter about the high cost of health care.
3. Two middle-income people in the United States are discussing the high cost of health care.
4. An insurance salesperson is explaining to a reporter why the cost of medical insurance is so high.
5. A doctor is telling a patient why medical bills are so high.
6. Two doctors are arguing about national health care; one is for it, one against.
7. A person from Britain (or Sweden, or Russia, or your native country) is talking with a person from the United States about whose health care system is better.
8. A doctor from the United States and one from another country (you choose which one) are discussing whose health care system is better.
9. A doctor is explaining to a group of United States government representatives (which can be the whole class) the advantages of national health care. The representatives will then ask questions.
10. A doctor who cares about doctor-patient relationships is speaking sympathetically to a patient who has a sickness.
11. A doctor who doesn't care about doctor-patient relationships is speaking quickly to a line of patients, taking just a few minutes for each person.

IX FOR DISCUSSION AND COMPOSITION

Choose one of the following to discuss or write about.

1. Describe the system of health care in the United States. Is it good? Why?
2. Describe the system of health care in your native country. Is it good? Why?
3. Compare the systems of health care in the United States and in your native country.
4. Why does health care in the United States cost a lot of money?
5. Discuss the advantages and disadvantages of private health care.
6. Discuss the advantages and disadvantages of government health care.
7. Which is better—private health care or government health care? Why?
8. Discuss how the system of health care in the United States or in your native country could be improved.
9. Describe the health care you have received in your life. Has it been good? Why?
10. Do you know anyone who had a serious illness? Did he or she receive good health care? Describe it.
11. Describe the experiences you have had recently with doctors. Have they been good? Why?
12. Describe the experiences you have had with hospitals. Have they been good? Why?

MEN AND WOMEN

WHY I WANT A WIFE: A WOMAN'S VIEW

Judy Syfers

Ms. Syfers points out that it is most convenient to have a wife. A wife will take care of your children, cook your food, clean and mend your clothes, entertain your friends, and so on. Certainly, anyone would want to have a wife. The only trouble is, who would want to be a wife?

1. I belong to the group of people known as wives. I am a wife. And partly as a result of that, I am a mother.

2. Not too long ago, a male friend of mine, who had just gotten divorced, visited me from the Midwest. He had one child, who is, of
5 course, with his ex-wife.° He was clearly looking for another wife. As I thought about him while I was ironing one evening, I suddenly realized that I, too, would like to have a wife. Why do I want a wife?

    former wife

3. I would like to go back to school so that I can become economically independent, support myself, and, if necessary, support those who are
10 dependent upon me. I want a wife who will work and send me to school, and, while I am going to school, take care of my children. I want a wife to remember the children's doctor's and dentist's appointments—and mine too. She must make sure my children eat properly and are kept clean, and wash and mend the children's clothes.
15 I want a wife who cares about my children, arranges for their schooling, makes sure they have a good social life, and takes them to

Adapted from "Why I Want a Wife" by Judy Syfers in *Ms.* (Spring 1972). Reprinted by permission of the author.

the park, the zoo, etc. I want a wife who takes care of the children when
they are sick, and who manages to be around when the children need
special care, because, of course, I cannot miss classes at school. She
20   must arrange to stay home from work without losing her job, even
though it may mean a small decrease in her salary from time to time.
Of course, my wife will arrange and pay for the care of the children
while she is working.

4.   I want a wife who will take care of my needs and keep my house
25   clean, who will pick up° after my children, and after me. I want a wife   **pick**...clean up
who will keep my clothes clean, ironed, mended, replaced when
necessary, and will make sure that my things are kept in their proper
place so that I can find what I need when I need it. She must be a good
cook, plan the menus, do the necessary grocery shopping, prepare the
30   meals, serve them well, and then clean up while I do my studying. I
want a wife who will take care of me when I am sick and sympathize
with° my pain and loss of time from school. She must go along when   **sympathize**...feel
our family takes a vacation so that someone can continue to take care of   sorry about
me and my children when I need a rest and a change of scene.

35   5.   I want a wife who will take care of the details of my social life.
When we are invited out by my friends, she will take care of the
babysitting arrangements. When I meet people at school that I like and
want to entertain, she will have the house clean, prepare a special meal,
serve it to me and my friends, and not interrupt when I talk about the
40   things that interest me and my friends. My wife will have arranged for
the children to be fed and ready for bed before my guests arrive so that
the children do not bother us. She will take care of the needs of my
guests, making sure that they feel comfortable, that they have an
ashtray, that they are passed the hors d'oeuvres,° that they are offered a   **hors**...food served
45   second helping of the food, that their wine glasses are filled when   before a meal
necessary, that their coffee is served to them as they like it. And I want a
wife who knows that sometimes I need a night out by myself.

6.   If, by chance, I find another person more satisfactory as a wife than
the wife I already have, I want the freedom to replace my present wife
50   with another one. Naturally, I will expect a fresh, new life; my wife
will take the children and be responsible for them so that I am left free.

7.   My God, who wouldn't want a wife?

Useful Words and Expressions

introduction   have a wife
   convenient   cook

clean
mend
certainly
paragraph 1
  wives
  as a result
  mother
paragraph 2
  male friend
  gotten divorced
  child
  of course
  ex-wife
paragraph 3
  go back to school
  economically independent
  support
  dependent
  doctor and dentist appointments
  make sure
  eat properly
  etc.
  manages
  be around
  decrease
  salary
  from time to time

paragraph 4
  take care of
  pick up
  in their proper place
  plan the menus
  do the grocery shopping
  prepare the meals
  sick
  sympathize
paragraph 5
  social life
  babysitting arrangements
  entertain
  a special meal
  children
  bother
  hors d'oeuvres
  a night out
  by myself
paragraph 6
  by chance
  more satisfactory
  freedom
  replace my wife
  be responsible for the children
  free

• • • • • E•X•E•R•C•I•S•E•S • • • • •

I READING COMPREHENSION

1. What is the main idea of the article?
  a. It is very convenient to have a wife.
  b. Many wives are mothers.
  c. Ms. Syfers is happy that she is a wife.

2. Ms. Syfers' male friend in paragraph 2
  a. had been divorced for a long time
  b. had his child with him
  c. wanted a new wife

3. Ms. Syfers wants a wife who
    a. will stay home and take care of the children
    b. will both work and take care of the children
    c. wants to have a good social life

4. Her wife may have to stay home from work because
    a. Ms. Syfers cannot miss classes at school
    b. The wife will be very tired
    c. The wife may lose her job

5. The wife must go on vacaion sometimes
    a. because she is tired
    b. because she will enjoy it
    c. to take care of Ms. Syfers

6. During a party, the wife should
    a. talk about what she is interested in
    b. not interrupt when Ms. Syfers is talking
    c. have a good time

7. If Ms. Syfers finds a more satisfactory wife
    a. the first wife should take the children
    b. the first wife should be upset
    c. Ms. Syfers should take the children

8. In this article, Ms. Syfers
    a. really means just what she says
    b. suggests it is unpleasant to be a wife
    c. suggests it is good to be a wife

II VOCABULARY

From the list of words below, choose the correct word for each blank space. Use each word only once.

sympathize	manages	appointments
properly	responsible	arrangements
etc.	menus	special
dependent	entertain	bother

1. I would like to go back to school so that I can support those who are
   dependent upon me.
2. I want a wife to remember the children's doctor's and dentist's _appointments_
3. She must make sure my children eat _properly_ .
4. I want a wife who takes the children to the park, the zoo, _____ .

5. I want a wife who _makesure_ to be around when the children need special care.
6. She must be a good cook, plan the _menu_, do the shopping, prepare the meals, and serve them well.
7. I want a wife who will take care of me when I am sick and _social life_ with my pain.
8. When we are invited out, she will take care of the babysitting _arrangements_
9. My wife will have arranged for the children to be ready for bed so that they do not _bother_ us.
10. My wife will take the children and be _responsible_ for them so that I am left free.

III PREPOSITIONS

Fill in the correct preposition for each blank space.

1. I belong _to_ the group _with_ people known _____ wives.
2. I want a wife who cares _for_ my children, arranges _for_ their schooling, and takes them _to_ the park, the zoo, etc.
3. She must arrange to stay home _to_ work _lost_ losing her job, even though it may mean a small decrease _on_ her salary _from_ time _to_ time.
4. _Of_ course, my wife will arrange and pay _for_ the care _____ the children while she is working.
5. I want a wife who will take care _of_ me when I am sick and sympathize _with_ my pain and loss _of_ time _from_ school.
6. She must go along when our family takes a vacation so that someone can continue to take care _of_ me when I need a rest and a change _of_ scene.
7. When I meet people _at_ school that I like and want to entertain, she will prepare a special meal, serve it _to_ me and my friends, and not interrupt when I talk _about_ the things that interest me and my friends.
8. If, _by_ chance, I find another person more satisfactory _as_ a wife than the wife I already have, I want the freedom to replace my present wife _with_ another one.

IV COMMON EXPRESSIONS

Choose the correct expression for each blank space.

social life	– as a result	– economically independent
– of course	– make sure	– from time to time
– do the grocery shopping	– hors d'oeuvres	– by myself
in their proper place	– by chance	be around

1. I am a wife, and, partly _____ of that, I am a mother.
2. My friend has one child, who is, _____, with his ex-wife.
3. I would like to go back to school so that I can become _____.
4. My wife must _____ my children eat properly.
5. She must arrange to stay home from work, even though it may mean a small decrease in her salary _____.
6. She must be a good cook, plan the menus, _____, prepare the meals, and serve them well.
7. I want a wife who will take care of the details of my _____.
8. She will take care of the needs of my guests, making sure that they feel comfortable, that they are passed the _____, that their coffee is served to them as they like it.
9. I want a wife who knows that sometimes I need a night out _____.
10. If, _____, I find another person more satisfactory as a wife, I want the freedom to replace my present wife with another one.

V DEFINITE/INDEFINITE ARTICLES

Use *a/an* or *the* where needed. If no article is needed, write an X in the blank space.

I would like to go back to _____ school so that I can become economically independent, support myself, and, if necessary support those who are dependent upon me. I want _____ wife who will work and send me to _____ school, and, while I am going to _____ school, take care of my children. I want _____ wife to remember _____ children's doctor's and dentist's appointments—and mine too. She must make sure my children eat properly and are kept clean, and wash and mend _____ children's clothes. I want _____ wife who cares about my children, arranges for their schooling, makes sure they have _____ good social life, and takes them to _____ park, _____ zoo, etc.

VI WORD FORMS

verbs	nouns	adjectives and participles	adverbs
A. depend	dependence independence	dependent independent	independently
B. support	support	supportive	supportively
C. specialize	specialty specialist	special	especially
D. lose	loss	lost	
E. sympathize	sympathy	sympathetic	sympathetically
F. entertain	entertainment entertainer	entertaining entertained	

verbs	nouns	adjectives and participles	adverbs
G.	comfort	comfortable uncomfortable	comfortably
H.	responsibility irresponsibility	responsible irresponsible	responsibly irresponsibly

Use the correct word in the sentences below.

A. depend, dependence, independence, dependent, independent, independently
  1. July 4 in the United States is _____ day.
  2. On that day, the United States declared itself to be an _____ country.
  3. Many women _____ on their husbands.
  4. Often, the women are unhappy about this _____.
  5. They would not be so _____ if they had good jobs.
  6. Mr. Jones has so much money that he is _____ wealthy.
B. support, support, supportive, supportively
  1. I hope you will give me your _____ with this plan.
  2. I _____ your plan last year.
  3. You have always been _____ to me.
  4. You spoke to me _____ about this yesterday.
C. specialize, specialty, specialist, special, especially
  1. The _____ of this restaurant is moussaka.
  2. It's really a very _____ dish.
  3. A _____ is someone who _____ in a particular kind of medicine.
  4. You should hurry up, _____ if you want to be on time.
D. lose, loss, lost
  1. I saw a sign about a _____ cat yesterday.
  2. It is upsetting to _____ something that you like.
  3. Sam's company suffered a great financial _____ last year.
E. sympathize, sympathy, sympathetic, sympathetically
  1. Mary listened to me _____ last night.
  2. She _____ with my problem.
  3. I appreciate her _____.
  4. She really is a very _____ person.
F. entertain, entertainment, entertainer, entertaining, entertained
  1. The comedian last night was very _____.
  2. He has been an _____ for a long time.
  3. The audience was well _____.
  4. It is a great talent to be able to _____ others.
  5. New York is sometimes called the _____ capital of the world.
G. comfort, comfortable, uncomfortable, comfortably
  1. I love this house; it's very _____ to live here.

2. We were very _____ when we lived in a small apartment.

3. You can sit very _____ in this car.

4. A lot of small cars are not built for _____.

H. responsibility, irresponsibility, responsible, irresponsible, responsibly, irresponsibly

1. Jack is always late for work; he's very _____.

2. The other employees where Jack works behave more _____.

3. He had better behave more _____ or else he will lose his job for his _____.

4. Wives are usually _____ for their children.

5. Husbands should share this _____.

VII   VALUES DISCUSSION

Answer the following questions. Then discuss your answers with your classmates.

1. What is the worst thing about being a wife?
   a. having to take care of children
   b. having to take care of a husband
   c. having to clean the house
   d. other

2. What is the best thing about being a wife?
   a. Your husband loves you.
   b. Your children love you.
   c. Other people in society respect you.
   d. other

3. How do husbands usually treat their wives?
   a. very well
   b. badly
   c. well enough
   d. other

4. How do wives usually treat their husbands?
   a. very well
   b. badly
   c. well enough
   d. other

5. Who should take care of children?
   a. the wife
   b. the husband

    c. a babysitter
    d. other

6. Should women work outside the home?
    a. yes
    b. no
    c. if the family needs the money
    d. other

7. Most men get married because
    a. they need someone to cook their food
    b. they want someone to have their children
    c. their parents want them to
    d. other

8. Most women get married because
    a. they need someone to make money for them
    b. they don't want to live with their parents
    c. they want to have children
    d. other

9. How are women's lives compared to men's lives?
    a. better
    b. worse
    c. the same
    d. other

10. What kind of life do wives in your native country have?
    a. very good
    b. very bad
    c. good enough
    d. other

11. What kind of life do wives in your native country have compared to wives in the United States?
    a. better
    b. worse
    c. the same
    d. other

12. How do you feel about women's liberation?
    a. It is very good.
    b. It is very bad.
    c. It is not necessary.
    d. other

VIII   ROLEPLAYING

Choose one of the following situations to act out.

1. A wife is telling a husband why she is unhappy about what she has to do in their marriage.
2. A married man is explaining to an unmarried male friend why it is good to be married.
3. A married woman is telling an unmarried female friend why she should not get married.
4. A women is complaining to her mother about what her husband expects her to do.
5. A man is telling his wife why his life is just as hard as hers.
6. A group of married women are discussing why they are dissatisfied with being married.
7. A woman from your native country is telling an American woman about marriage in your native country.
8. A liberated woman is telling an unliberated woman what she should do to make her life better.
9. A liberated woman is talking to a group (which can be the whole class) about what women should do to improve their lives.

IX   FOR DISCUSSION AND COMPOSITION

Choose one of the following to discuss or write about.

1. Why is it pleasant to have a wife?
2. What are a wife's responsibilities?
3. What are a husband's responsibilities?
4. Does a wife have a difficult life? Why?
5. Does a husband have a difficult life? Why?
6. Who has a more difficult life, a wife or a husband? Why?
7. Describe the role of a particular wife that you know. Is she happy? Why?
8. Describe the kind of wife that your mother was. Was she happy? Why?
9. Describe the role of wives in your native country.
10. Would you rather be a wife in your native country or in the United States? Why?
11. Describe the differences between wives in the past and today (either in the United States or in your native country).
12. Write an essay called "Why I Want a Husband," discussing how life can be very easy if you have a husband.

MEN'S LIVES

Len Fox

I agree with Ms. Syfers (see the previous article, p. 85) that there are many things about the traditional role of a wife that are both unpleasant and unfair. She seems to suggest, however, that men's lives are very pleasant. With this, I disagree. In fact, I think that women's lives are probably, on the whole°, more pleasant and satisfying than those of men. For their own good, men in American society should try to change their way of life. We need not only women's liberation, but also men's liberation.

on...in most cases

1. Many women in America feel that men have a better deal° in our society than women do. When you look carefully at men's lives though, you may begin to wonder about that.

have...have a better situation

2. The difference begins with babies. Male babies are picked up, hugged,° and talked to less. Even at this age, they are beginning to learn to be independent and to not need to be comforted when something bothers them. The trouble is, it's nice to be hugged and talked to. Male babies are missing out on° something important.

held with arms around

missing...not getting

3. Little boys continue to learn how to be "a real man." They are told that boys should not cry. Of course, it's natural to cry if you are hurt. So little boys try not to pay attention to how they feel. Later on, they will try to ignore other "feminine" feelings such as doubt or sadness. The boys will get so good at this that they may eventually° not be aware of having any feelings at all.

after some time

15   **4.**   Another important lesson for little boys is learned in sports. They
see that people admire boys who are good in sports, so they try to work
hard to be better than everyone else. If a friend is very good in sports, a
boy will feel threatened,° since the friend will appear more "manly,"   in danger
and thus better than he is. This doesn't encourage very close, warm
20 feelings of friendship.

5.   When boys become men, the competition that they experienced in
sports is now found in their work. A man is usually respected if he
earns a lot of money, so men do their best to continually get ahead,°   **get**...move up
trying to be better than their "friends" at work. Then they will be the
25 one to get that all important promotion.° Many men have jobs that   change to a more
they dislike and that do not allow them to use any creativity or natural   important job
ability that they may have. But work is not to enjoy; it is a way to prove
that you are really a man.

6.   A man may have gotten married and may have children, but he is
30 often too busy working to spend much time with his family. His wife
has to work hard at home, and perhaps outside the home as well, but at
least raising children is rewarding work. The children will love their
mother and the close relationship between them will last throughout
their lives. All too often, the children don't even feel that they know
35 their father very well. The father seems to be at work all the time. Even
when he's at home, his years of repressing° his feelings and distrusting   holding in
others have not taught him how to communicate° with people very   share or exchange
well. He just seems to be the "strong, silent type."   feelings, information

7.   So what exactly is there to envy about the life of a man? True, men
40 have more positions of power in this country, and women should be
given equal opportunities to obtain such positions. But that is hardly a
reason to envy men. If their personal lives are unhappy, they are more
to be pitied than envied.

8.   Hopefully, the roles° of women and men will change in our   parts, expected actions
45 society. Just as women should learn to be more assertive,° self-   forceful
confident, and independent, men should learn to be more gentle,
trusting, able to listen and to share. The happiest people will be those
who have developed both the masculine and feminine sides of
themselves.

Useful Words and Expressions

introduction	men's lives
wife	pleasant
unpleasant	satisfying
unfair	men's liberation

paragraph 1
  have a better deal
  wonder
paragraph 2
  difference
  babies
  picked up
  hugged
  talked to
  be comforted
  something bothers them
paragraph 3
  a real man
  cry
  hurt
  pay attention to
  ignore
  feminine feelings
  aware
  at all
paragraph 4
  sports
  admire
  be good in
  work hard
  be better
  threatened
  manly
paragraph 5
  competition
  work
  earn a lot of money
  get ahead

promotion
dislike
creativity
prove
paragraph 6
  busy
  spend time
  raising children
  rewarding
  mother
  close relationship
  father
  repressing his feelings
  distrusting
  communicate
paragraph 7
  envy
  positions of power
  equal opportunities
  personal lives
  unhappy
paragraph 8
  roles
  women
  assertive
  self-confident
  independent
  men
  gentle
  trusting
  listen
  share
  masculine and feminine sides

• • • • • E • X • E • R • C • I • S • E • S • • • • •

I READING COMPREHENSION

1. What is the main idea of the article?
    a. There are many bad things about men's lives.

    b. Men have a better life than women.

    c. Males are independent.

2. What is not true about male babies?
    a. They learn to be independent.
    b. They are talked to less.
    c. They are not missing anything.

3. Little boys feel that "a real man"
    a. does not cry
    b. has strong feelings
    c. feels a lot of doubt

4. In sports
    a. boys want their friends to be good
    b. boys feel very friendly with the other players
    c. boys want to be better than their friends

5. In their jobs, most men
    a. love what they are doing
    b. work for a promotion
    c. use a lot of creativity

6. Children usually
    a. feel close to their father
    b. spend a lot of time with their father
    c. love their mother

7. Men are usually all the following except
    a. assertive
    b. gentle
    c. independent

8. The author feels that
    a. men do not have good qualities
    b. men should not be feminine
    c. men should have both feminine and masculine qualities

II VOCABULARY

From the list of words below, choose the correct word for each blank space. Use each word only once.

promotion	repressing	aware
hugged	envy	roles

share   equal   creativity
threatened   sides   assertive

1. Male babies are picked up, _____, and talked to less.
2. The boys will get so good at ignoring feelings that they may not be _____ of having any feelings at all.
3. If a friend is very good in sports, a boy will feel _____.
4. Men do their best to get ahead, trying to be better than their "friends" at work. Then they will be the one to get that all important _____.
5. The man's years of _____ his feelings and distrusting others have not taught him how to communicate with people very well.
6. Women should be given _____ opportunities to obtain positions of power.
7. Hopefully, the _____ of women and men will change in our society.
8. Women should learn to be more _____, self-confident, and independent.
9. Men should learn to be more gentle, trusting, able to listen and to _____.
10. The happiest people will be those who have developed both the masculine and feminine _____ of themselves.

III   PREPOSITIONS

Fill in the correct preposition for each blank space.

1. Many women _____ America feel that men have a better deal _____ our society than women do.
2. The difference begins _____ babies. Male babies are picked _____, hugged, and talked _____ less.
3. The boys will get so good _____ ignoring feelings that they may eventually not be aware _____ having any feelings _____ all.
4. Another important lesson _____ little boys is learned _____ sports.
5. The wife has to work hard _____ home, and perhaps _____ the home as well, but _____ least raising children is rewarding work.
6. The children will love their mother and the close relationship _____ them will last _____ their lives.
7. Even when the father is _____ home, his years _____ repressing his feelings have not taught him how to communicate _____ people very well.
8. Hopefully, the roles _____ women and men will change _____ our society.

IV   COMMON EXPRESSIONS

Choose the correct expression for each blank space.

are good in	have a better deal	spend time
be comforted	pay attention to	self-confident
close relationship	a real man	get ahead
raising children	work hard	at all

1. Many women in America feel that men _____ in our society.
2. Even as babies, males are beginning to learn to be independent and to not need to _____ when something bothers them.
3. Little boys continue to learn how to be _____.
4. They will get so good at ignoring feelings that they may eventually not be aware of having any feelings _____.
5. People admire boys who _____ sports.
6. Boys try to _____ to be better than everyone else.
7. A man is usually respected if he earns a lot of money, so men do their best to _____.
8. The father is too busy working to _____ with his family.
9. The children will love their mother and the _____ between them will last throughout their lives.
10. Women should learn to be more assertive, _____, and independent.

V DEFINITE/INDEFINITE ARTICLES

Use *a/an* or *the* where needed. If no article is needed, write an X in the blank space.

_____ man may have gotten married and may have _____ children, but he is often too busy working to spend much time with his family. His wife has to work hard at _____ home, and perhaps outside _____ home as well, but at least raising _____ children is _____ rewarding work. _____ children will love their mother and _____ close relationship between them will last throughout their lives. All too often, _____ children don't even feel that they know their father very well. _____ father seems to be at _____ work all _____ time. Even when he's at _____ home, his years of repressing his feelings and distrusting others have not taught him how to communicate with _____ people very well. He just seems to be _____ "strong, silent type."

VI WORD FORMS

	verbs	nouns	adjectives and participles	adverbs
A.	doubt	doubt	doubtful	undoubtedly
B.		sadness	sad	sadly
C.	admire	admiration	admirable	admirably
D.	threaten	threat	threatened	
			threatening	threateningly

	verbs	nouns	adjectives and participles	adverbs
E.		friend	friendly	
		friendship	unfriendly	
F.	know	knowledge	knowledgeable	knowledgeably
G.		power	powerful	powerfully
			powerless	
H.		happiness	happy	happily
			unhappy	

Use the correct word in the sentences below.

A. doubt, doubt, doubtful, undoubtedly
   1. George feels _____ about getting into college.
   2. _____, he will be accepted by a good college because he is a good student.
   3. I don't know why he feels so much _____.
   4. I _____ that he will have any trouble.

B. sadness, sad, sadly
   1. The child looked at her mother _____ when the mother left home.
   2. The child was _____ because her mother was going away.
   3. _____ in children usually doesn't last long.

C. admire, admiration, admirable, admirably
   1. I feel a lot of _____ for Dr. Jones.
   2. I _____ the work he has done.
   3. He does his job _____.
   4. I would like to be such an _____ person.

D. threaten, threat, threatened, threatening, threateningly
   1. The robber spoke to the man _____.
   2. The man felt very _____.
   3. A _____ experience like that is very upsetting.
   4. My boss made a _____ to fire me if I don't come to work on time.
   5. He _____ his employees all the time.

E. friend, friendship, friendly, unfriendly
   1. I like Jane because she is a _____ person.
   2. She was _____ last night, though; perhaps she wasn't feeling well.
   3. She has been a _____ of mine since I was a child.
   4. I value her _____.

F. know, knowledge, knowledgeable, knowledgeably
   1. Dr. Brown _____ a lot about biology.
   2. He is considered a very _____ person in his field.
   3. It must have taken him a long time to acquire so much _____.
   4. He always lectures very _____.

G. power, powerful, powerless, powerfully
   1. Mr. Williams is a very _____ man.

2. He always states his opinions _____.
3. Many people envy him because of his _____.
4. Although I saw a car heading towards mine, I was _____ to avoid an accident.

H. happiness, happy, unhappy, happily
1. The child was playing _____.
2. Children are usually _____.
3. Adults are often _____ because they worry about a lot of things.
4. Money can't buy _____.

VII   VALUES DISCUSSION

Answer the following questions. Then discuss your answers with your classmates.

1. What is the worst thing about men's lives?
   a. Men don't feel free to be emotional and express their feelings.
   b. Men feel they have to compete all the time.
   c. Most men don't have a good family life.
   d. other

2. How do you feel about the way boys and girls should be raised?
   a. Boys should be allowed to do things that girls do.
   b. Boys should not be allowed to do things that girls do.
   c. The way boys and girls are raised now is fine.
   d. other

3. What do you think about the effect of sports on boys?
   a. Sports have a good effect.
   b. Sports have a bad effect.
   c. Sports have more bad effects than good ones.
   d. other

4. How do you feel about competition?
   a. Competition is good.
   b. Competition is bad.
   c. Competition is necessary.
   d. other

5. How do you think most men feel about their jobs?
   a. Most men like their jobs.
   b. Most men dislike their jobs.
   c. Most men only care about the money they make on their jobs.
   d. other

6. What do you think about the amount of time most men spend with their families?
   a. Most men spend enough time.

    b. Most men don't spend enough time.

    c. Men should spend most of their time at work.

    d. other

7. What do you think of the lives of men in your native country compared to the lives of men in the United States?

    a. Men in my native country have a better life.

    b. Men in the United States have a better life.

    c. The lives of men in my native country are very different from the lives of men in the United States.

    d. other

8. How do you feel about men's lives compared to women's lives?

    a. Men have better lives.

    b. Women have better lives.

    c. Men's lives are the same as women's lives.

    d. other

9. The best quality that men have is being

    a. assertive

    b. self-confident

    c. independent

    d. other

10. The best quality that women have is being

    a. gentle

    b. trusting

    c. able to listen

    d. other

11. How do you feel about men and "feminine qualities"?

    a. Men should have more feminine qualities.

    b. Men should not have feminine qualities.

    c. There is no such thing as feminine qualities.

    d. other

12. How do you feel about women and "masculine qualities"?

    a. Women should have more masculine qualities.

    b. Women should not have masculine qualities.

    c. There is no such thing as masculine qualities.

    d. other

VIII ROLEPLAYING

Choose one of the following situations to act out.

1. A man is telling a woman why he wants to be a strong, dominant ("macho") type of person. The woman tells him why he shouldn't be that way.

2. Two men in the United States are discussing why their lives are very difficult.

3. A man from your native country and a man from the United States are comparing the types of lives that men have in the two places.

4. One parent is telling another why boys should be allowed to play with dolls and girls should be allowed to play with cars. The second parent disagrees.

5. A man is explaining to a woman why he sometimes thinks it would be nice to be a woman, and the woman is explaining why she sometimes would like to be a man.

6. Two men are discussing what they like and dislike about women.

7. Two women are discussing what they like and dislike about men.

8. A man who likes to play sports and one who doesn't are explaining to each other why they feel as they do.

9. A person who thinks competition is good is arguing with someone who thinks it is bad.

10. An adult is telling a little boy that it's fine to cry if he feels sad or if he gets hurt. The little boy isn't sure about this.

11. A man who wants to get a promotion at work is arguing with a friend who doesn't care about getting promotions.

12. A wife is telling her husband why he should spend more time at home.

IX   FOR DISCUSSION AND COMPOSITION

Choose one of the following to discuss or write about.

1. What are some unpleasant things about the lives of men in the United States? Mention competition, the lack of family life, the tendency to not express feelings, and so on.

2. What causes men to develop as they do? Mention how babies are treated, how parents treat boys compared to girls, the toys that boys play with, and so on.

3. In many countries, boys are encouraged to play with toy cars, but not with dolls, while girls are encouraged to play with dolls, but not toy cars. Is this good? Why?

4. Discuss the advantages and disadvantages of being a man.

5. Discuss the advantages and disadvantages of being a woman.

6. (For men) Do you have any "feminine qualities"? Is this good? Why?

7. (For women) Do you have any "masculine qualities"? Is this good? Why?

8. Compare men in your native country and men in the United States. Who has a better life? Why?

9. Discuss good and bad attitudes that people develop through sports.

10. Is there much competition between men in your native country? Is this good? Why?

11. Do men in your native country have close friendships with other men? Discuss and provide examples.

12. In this article, the writer is suggesting that men should be more "feminine" and that women should be more "masculine." Do you agree? Why?

THROWAWAY MARRIAGES: A THREAT* TO THE AMERICAN FAMILY?

As has been mentioned in the two previous articles, changes are occurring in the roles of men and women in our society. Partly as a result of these changes, a great deal of stress° is placed on modern   pressure
v *marriages. When a married couple is unable to deal with this stress, the result is divorce.°*   ending a marriage

1. The United States divorce rate, arriving at a new high in 1974, shows this fact: divorce and remarriage—what some people call "serial marriages" and others describe as "throwaway marriages"—have become part of American society and are spreading fast. Today, 21
5 percent of all married couples in the United States have divorce somewhere in the background of one partner or another or both. Divorces are becoming so common that Paul C. Glick, who works in the Census Bureau's population department, said that among today's thirty-year-old wives, about one out of every three marriages has been
10 or will be ended by divorce. In fact, unless something is done to stop divorce, says Mr. Glick, more than 40 percent of all marriages may end in this way. This spread° of divorce is bringing great economic and   increase
social change to the United States.

2. For the man, divorce can mean months, even years, of alimony°   payments to an ex-wife
15 and child-support payments—although most men, after a while, stop

* sign of danger

Adapted from *U.S. News & World Report* (January 13, 1975).

making the payments regularly. For the woman, divorce may mean
finding a job, perhaps for the first time in her life, and learning to live
on the income—which for women is usually only three-fifths of male
income. More than ten million children are now living with only one
20 parent, and two out of three of these are the product of divorce or
separation.

3.   Many Americans are worried about the divorce rate, just as they are
about the tendency for people to live together without getting married.
These traditional people—including many younger Americans—feel
25 that marriage should keep people together "till death do us part." But
others accept divorce as an inevitable° product of many things—   necessary, unavoidable
including the women's rights movement, new attitudes about sex, the
difficulties of urban living,° and the weakening of religion as a   **urban**...living in cities
controlling force. Furthermore, it is pointed out that the high rate of
30 remarriage after divorce might be a sign of the continuing strength of
marriage and family.

4.   To avoid divorce, more and more couples are looking for help from
ministers, doctors, marriage counselors, and sex therapists. Often,
however, couples put off seeking help until it is too late to save the
35 marriage. It will be a long time, say social scientists, before Americans
find a way to reduce divorce rates—or to deal satisfactorily with the
problems that divorce represents in family life.

Copyright 1975 U.S. News & World Report, Inc.

Useful Words and Expressions

introduction	after a while
changes	stop
stress	woman
marriages	finding a job
paragraph 1	for the first time
divorce rate	income
divorce	children
common	separation
be ended	*paragraph 3*
something is done	worried
spread	tendency
social change	live together
paragraph 2	getting married
man	traditional
alimony	till death do us part
child support	accept
although	inevitable

the women's rights movement marriage counselors
urban living seeking help
pointed out a long time
remarriage reduce divorce rates
paragraph 4 deal with
avoid problems
more and more

• • • • •E •X •E •R •C •I •S •E •S• • • • •

I READING COMPREHENSION

1. What is the main idea of the article?
   a. Divorce and remarriage is called "serial marriage."
   b. Many children today are living with only one parent.
   c. Divorce is becoming increasingly common in the United States.

2. According to Paul C. Glick
   a. one out of three thirty-year-old wives in the United States today has gotten or
      will get divorced
   b. one out of three thirty-year-old women in the United States is divorced
   c. 40 percent of all marriages in the United States have ended in divorce

3. According to the article, divorce is difficult for women because
   a. they must pay alimony
   b. they usually receive lower salaries than men
   c. they are happier when they are married

4. In the United States today
   a. everyone is worried about the divorce rate
   b. everyone accepts the divorce rate
   c. some accept divorce as a necessary result of our changing society

5. The increased divorce rate is caused by all of the following except
   a. the high rate of remarriage
   b. the women's rights movement
   c. the difficulties of urban living

6. The high rate of remarriage after divorce might show
   a. that divorce will become more common
   b. that people still want to be married
   c. that the family will not last as a social institution

7. According to the article, many couples today
    a. didn't want to get married in the first place
    b. have financial problems
    c. put off seeking help until it is too late

8. Put the following sentences in the correct order
    a. These traditional people feel that marriage should keep people together "till death do us part."
    b. Furthermore, it is pointed out that the high rate of remarriage might be a sign of the strength of marriage and family.
    c. Many Americans are worried about the divorce rate.
    d. But others accept divorce as an inevitable product of many things.

II VOCABULARY

From the list of words below, choose the correct word for each blank space. Use each word only once.

avoid	spread	reduce
traditional	common	seeking
income	although	inevitable
divorce	separation	tendency

1. Today, 21 percent of all married couples in the United States have _____ somewhere in the background of one partner or another or both.
2. Divorces are becoming so _____ that among today's thirty-year-old wives, about one out of every three marriages has been or will be ended by divorce.
3. This _____ of divorce is bringing great economic and social change to the United States.
4. For the man, divorce can mean years of alimony, _____ most men, after a while, stop making the payments regularly.
5. For the woman, divorce may mean finding a job and learning to live on the _____.
6. Many Americans are worried about the _____ for people to live together without getting married.
7. These _____ people feel that marriage should keep people together "till death do us part."
8. Others accept divorce as an _____ product of many things.
9. To _____ divorce, more and more couples are looking for help.
10. It will be a long time before Americans find a way to _____ divorce rates.

III PREPOSITIONS

Fill in the correct preposition for each blank space.

1. The United States divorce rate, arriving _____ a new high in 1974, shows divorce and remarriage have become part _____ American society.
2. Today 21 percent _____ all married couples in the United States have divorce somewhere _____ the background of one partner or another or both.
3. _____ today's thirty-year-old wives, about one _____ _____ every three marriages has been or will be ended _____ divorce.
4. This spread _____ divorce is bringing great economic and social change _____ the United States.
5. _____ the man, divorce can mean years _____ alimony and child-support payments.
6. _____ the woman, divorce may mean finding a job, perhaps _____ the first time _____ her life.
7. Many Americans are worried _____ the divorce rate, just as they are _____ the tendency _____ people to live together _____ getting married.
8. Others accept divorce _____ an inevitable product _____ many things— including new attitudes _____ sex, the difficulties _____ urban living, and the weakening _____ religion.

IV COMMON EXPRESSIONS

Choose the correct expression for each blank space.

be ended	getting married	for the first time
after a while	more and more	live together
a long time	something is done	divorce rate
pointed out	social change	urban living

1. The United States _____ shows that divorce and remarriage are spreading fast.
2. Among today's thirty-year-old wives, about one out of every three marriages has been or will _____ by divorce.
3. Unless _____ to stop divorce, more than 40 percent of all marriages may end in this way.
4. This spread of divorce is bringing great economic and _____ to the United States.
5. Most men, _____, stop making child-support payments regularly.
6. For the woman, divorce may mean findng a job, perhaps _____ in her life.
7. Many Americans are worried about the tendency of people to live together without _____.

8. Others accept divorce as an inevitable product of many things, including the difficulties of _____ and the weakening of religion.
9. To avoid divorce, _____ couples are looking for help.
10. It will be _____ before Americans find a way to reduce divorce rates.

V   DEFINITE/INDEFINITE ARTICLES

Use *a/an* or *the* where needed. If no article is needed, write an X in the blank space.

Many Americans are worried about _____ divorce rate, just as they are about _____ tendency for _____ people to live together without getting married. These traditional people—including many younger Americans—feel that _____ marriage should keep _____ people together "till _____ death do us part." But others accept _____ divorce as _____ inevitable product of many things— including _____ women's rights movement, _____ new attitudes about _____ sex, _____ difficulties of urban living, and _____ weakening of _____ religion as _____ controlling force. Furthermore, it is pointed out that _____ high rate of _____ remarriage after _____ divorce might be _____ sign of _____ continuing strength of _____ marriage and _____ family.

VI   WORD FORMS

	verbs	nouns	adjectives and participles	adverbs
A.	socialize	society	social sociable	socially
B.	economize	economy	economic economical	economically
C.	worry	worry	worried	
D.	die	death	dead	deadly
E.	produce	product production	productive	productively
F.	weaken	weakness	weak	weakly
G.	help	help	helpful helpless	helpfully helplessly
H.	satisfy	satisfaction	satisfying satisfied	

Use the correct word in the sentences below.

A. socialize, society, social, sociable, socially
    1. There are many problems in American _____.

2. Americans must try to solve their _____ problems.
3. Mary likes to _____ with other people.
4. She is always very _____.
5. _____, she is a very pleasant person.

B. economize, economy, economics, economic, economical, economically
1. The United States has a strong _____.
2. The government tries to encourage _____ development.
3. The president recently made an _____ wise decision.
4. Since we don't have much money, we try to _____.
5. I try to be _____ when I go shopping.
6. Did you study _____ in school?

C. worry, worry, worried
1. Parents always have a lot of _____.
2. Sometimes they _____ about their children's education.
3. It is not good to be _____ all the time.

D. die, death, dead, deadly
1. Martin Luther King, Jr., is _____.
2. He _____ in 1968.
3. His _____ was a great loss to America.
4. A knife can be a _____ weapon.

E. produce, product, production, productive, productively
1. Oil is an important _____ of the Middle East.
2. The _____ of oil is important to all the countries in the world.
3. The United States _____ some oil.
4. Some of its oil fields are very _____.
5. Its companies are working _____ to increase oil supplies.

F. weaken, weakness, weak, weakly
1. John is very _____ right now.
2. His _____ is the result of his health.
3. The heart attack he had last month _____ him a great deal.
4. He can only speak _____.

G. help, help, helpful, helpless, helpfully, helplessly
1. The students gave the teachers a lot of _____ in preparing for the party.
2. They _____ decorated the room.
3. The teacher thanked them for being so _____.
4. You must _____ yourself.
5. I _____ watched the car accident occur; I hated feeling so _____.

H. satisfy, satisfaction, satisfying, satisfied
1. I get a lot of _____ out of my work.
2. I find it very _____.
3. When I come home at the end of the day, I feel _____.
4. You are lucky if your work _____ you.

VII VALUES DISCUSSION

Answer the following questions. Then discuss your answers with your classmates.

1. What, in your opinion, is the most important advantage of marriage?
   a. companionship (not being alone)
   b. being able to have children
   c. sharing work and money
   d. other

2. What is the greatest disadvantage of marriage?
   a. not being able to make friends of the opposite sex
   b. You fight with your husband or wife.
   c. You don't have much free time.
   d. other

3. What do you think is the most common reason for marriage?
   a. Young people don't want to live with their parents.
   b. Everybody else is doing it.
   c. People want to have sexual relations.
   d. other

4. In your opinion, what percentage of married people are happily married?
   a. 25 percent
   b. 50 percent
   c. 75 percent
   d. other

5. What do you think is the most common reason for divorce?
   a. A man is having a love affair with another woman.
   b. A woman is having a love affair with another man.
   c. The couple were too young when they got married.
   d. other

6. What is the worst disadvantage of getting divorced?
   a. Society disapproves of you.
   b. Your parents are upset.
   c. You feel like you have failed.
   d. other

7. How do you feel about the rising divorce rate?
   a. I think it's a good thing.
   b. I think it's a bad thing.
   c. I don't care.
   d. other

8. How do you feel about unmarried people living together?
   a. It's a good idea.
   b. It's a bad idea.
   c. Sometimes it's good.
   d. other

9. What should a married couple do to avoid divorce?
   a. They should go to a minister.
   b. They should go to a marriage counselor.
   c. They should speak to their parents.
   d. other

10. How does divorce affect children?
    a. It is bad for children.
    b. It is good for children.
    c. It doesn't affect them much.
    d. other

VIII   ROLEPLAYING

Choose one of the following situations to act out.

1. A person is explaining to a minister or marriage counselor why he or she wants to get divorced.
2. A person is explaining to one or both parents why he or she wants to get divorced.
3. A·person is telling a friend why he or she wants to get divorced.
4. A young person is talking to a friend and explaining why he or she wants to get married.
5. A married man or woman is telling the advantages and disadvantages of marriage to a young friend who is thinking about getting married.
6. Both parents are discussing with their child whether he or she is ready to get married.
7. A recently divorced person is telling a friend about the difficulties of being divorced.
8. A group of divorced people are discussing what they like and dislike about being divorced.
9. A group of married people are discussing what they like and dislike about being married.
10. A social scientist is explaining to an audience (which can be the whole class) why the divorce rate is rising. The audience can then ask questions.

IX   FOR DISCUSSION AND COMPOSITION

Choose one of the following to discuss or write about.

1. Explain why people get married.
2. Explain why people get divorced.
3. Is getting married a good idea? Why?
4. Is getting divorced a good idea? Why?
5. If you plan to get married, describe the kind of marriage you will want to have. (If you are married, describe the marriage you have.)

6. Describe the marriage of a couple that you know. Is it a good marriage? Why?
7. Do you know anyone who has gotten divorced? If so, explain why.
8. Describe an "ideal" (perfect) marriage.
9. Discuss how attitudes about mariage have changed in the last twenty years.
10. Discuss how attitudes about divorce have changed in the last twenty years.
11. Compare marriage in two different places (for example, in the United States and in your native country, or in the city and in the country areas of your nation).
12. What can a married couple do if they are having problems and are thinking about getting a divorce?

LIFE IN CITIES

RENOVATING*
OLD BUILDINGS

One of the most encouraging things happening in cities in the United States is that people are buying run-down° old buildings and changing them into very pleasant places to live. In some cases, as in Park Slope in Brooklyn, a whole area becomes a "renovation neighborhood" because a large number of people buy and fix up the old buildings. Thus a new appreciation of old buildings, which did not exist a decade° ago, is growing.

in bad condition

period of ten years

1. In cities across the United States, old factories, warehouses,° schools, railroad stations, and other buildings are being renovated for new uses. City planners and private investors° are finding that good buildings, no matter how old, can be remodeled for new purposes. "If you'd asked someone four or five years ago whether he'd rent an apartment in an abandoned° piano factory or clothing warehouse, he'd have thought you were crazy," says a New York architect.° "Today, many people are eager to do it." The renovating may include a former city hall or courthouse changed into offices; a bank or church changed into a restaurant; or, as in Plains, Georgia, a railroad station used as a center for a presidential campaign.

buildings to keep goods

people who buy something in order to make a profit

left alone, empty
person who plans buildings

2. Only a few decades ago, renovation was unpopular and generally far more expensive than taking down abandoned buildings and

* fixing, making new

Adapted from *U.S. News & World Report* (October 25, 1976).

starting from the beginning. A change began in the 1960s with a
15 number of well-advertised projects.° They included Ghirardelli Square   plans
in San Francisco, where an old chocolate factory was restored and made
into shops and restaurants; Trolley Square in Salt Lake City, where
abandoned car warehouses became a shopping mall;° the Soho district   **shopping**...a covered
of New York City, where unused warehouses were made into artists'   area with shops
20 studios and apartments.

3. What caused the change? "One reason is nostalgia,"° a San   feeling that the past is
Francisco builder suggests. "Maybe old is better than new, many   better
people are saying. Feelings about preserving attractive or historic
buildings have changed a great deal." A second cause is economic. The
25 cost of tearing down an old building and constructing a new one from
nothing now has risen to the point where it is often less expensive to fix
a solid older structure. Also builders realize that fixing up an existing
building often requires no new permits, zoning° changes, sewer lines,   rules about types of
or water connections.   buildings allowed in an
                                                                           area

30 **4.** Even when the costs of restoration are the same as or a bit more
than the costs of putting up a new building, fixing the old building
may be better. A Boston architect says, "The advantage comes when
you can develop a final project that is more desirable than a new
building—one with the right location, more space, more floor area, a
35 special character, materials of a particular quality." Gradually,
architects and builders are developing knowledge about renovation
and preservation, bringing imagination and creativity to the job.

Useful Words and Expressions

introduction   abandoned
   encouraging   crazy
   run-down old buildings   eager
   changing   changed into
   renovation neighborhood   offices
paragraph 1   *paragraph 2*
   warehouses   a few decades
   railroad stations   renovation
   renovated   expensive
   city planners   taking down
   private investors   abandoned buildings
   no matter how old   from the beginning
   new purposes   change
   rent an apartment   well advertised projects

paragraph 3	paragraph 4
cause	costs
nostalgia	restoration
feelings	more than
a great deal	advantage
cost	develop
to the point where	a final project
less expensive	desirable
builder	gradually
realize	knowledge
fixing up	
permits	

• • • • • •E•X•E•R•C•I•S•E•S• • • • • •

I READING COMPREHENSION

1. What is the main idea of the article?
   a. Renovating old buildings is becoming popular.
   b. Old buildings are better than new buildings.
   c. New buildings are better than old buildings.

2. Five years ago
   a. people were renting apartments in abandoned piano factories
   b. many people were eager to renovate buildings
   c. renovation was less popular than it is today

3. "Today many people are eager to do *it*." (paragraph 1.) *It* means
   a. abandon piano factories
   b. be crazy
   c. rent an apartment in an abandoned factory

4. A few decades ago
   a. renovation was popular
   b. building new buildings was more expensive than renovation
   c. renovation was more expensive than building new buildings

5. In the 1960s all the following occurred except
   a. an old chocolate factory was made into shops
   b. the Soho district of New York was made into warehouses
   c. abandoned car warehouses became a shopping mall

6. Renovation is becoming popular for all the following reasons except
    a. people do not want to preserve historic buildings
    b. it is more expensive to build a new building than it used to be
    c. new buildings require new permits, zoning changes, and so on

7. Fixing old buildings is good because it can result in all the following except
    a. more space
    b. inferior materials
    c. more floor area

8. Put the following in the correct order.
    a. They included Ghirardelli Square in San Francisco, Trolley Square in Salt Lake City, and the Soho district in New York City.
    b. A change began in the 1960s with a number of well-advertised projects.
    c. Only a few decades ago, renovation was unpopular.

II VOCABULARY

From the list of words below, choose the correct word for each blank space. Use each word only once.

nostalgia	warehouses	investors
realize	eager	develop
decades	final	rent
gradually	abandoned	purposes

1. In cities across the United States, old factories, _____, schools, and other buildings are being renovated for new uses.
2. City planners and private _____ are finding that good buildings can be remodeled for new purposes.
3. If you had asked someone four or five years ago whether he would _____ an apartment in an _____ piano factory, he would have thought you were crazy. Today many people are _____ to do it.
4. Only a few _____ ago, renovation was unpopular.
5. What caused the change? One reason is _____. "Maybe old is better than new, many people are saying."
6. Builders _____ that fixing up an existing building requires no new permits, zoning changes, and so on.
7. The advantage comes when you can develop a _____ project that is more desirable than a new building—one with the right location, more space, materials of a particular quality.
8. _____, architects and builders are developing knowledge about renovation and preservation.

III PREPOSITIONS

Fill in the correct preposition for each blank space.

1. _____ cities _____ the United States, old factories, warehouses, schools, and other buildings are being renovated _____ new uses.
2. The renovating may include a bank or church changed _____ a restaurant or, as _____ Plains, Georgia, a railroad station used _____ a center _____ a presidential campaign.
3. A change began _____ the 1960s _____ a number _____ well-advertised projects.
4. The projects included Ghirardelli Square _____ San Francisco, where an old chocolate factory was made _____ shops, and the Soho district _____ New York City, where unused warehouses were made _____ artists' studios and apartments.
5. The cost _____ tearing _____ an old building has risen _____ the point where it is often less expensive to fix a solid older structure.
6. Even when the costs _____ restoration are the same _____ or a bit more than the costs _____ putting _____ a new building, fixing the old building may be better.
7. The advantage comes when you can develop a final project that is more desirable than a new building—one _____ the right location, more space, materials _____ a particular quality.
8. Gradually, architects and builders are developing knowledge _____ renovation, bringing imagination and creativity _____ the job.

IV COMMON EXPRESSIONS

Choose the correct expression for each blank space.

to the point where	taking down	city planners
no matter	from the beginning	more than
well-advertised	railroad stations	changed into
fixing up	abandoned buildings	a great deal

1. _____ and private investors are finding that good buildings, _____ how old, can be remodeled for new purposes.
2. The renovating may include a former city hall or courthouse _____ offices, or a railroad station used as a center for a presidential campaign.
3. Only a few decades ago, renovation was unpopular and generally far more expensive than _____ an abandoned building and starting _____ .
4. A change began in the 1960s with a number of _____ projects.
5. Feelings about preserving attractive or historic buildings have changed _____ .

6. The cost of tearing down an old building and constructing a new one has risen _____ it is often less expensive to fix a solid older structure.

7. Also, builders realize that _____ an existing building often requires no new permits, zoning changes, and so on.

8. Even when the costs of restoration are the same as or a bit _____ the costs of putting up a new building, fixing the old building may be better.

V   DEFINITE/INDEFINITE ARTICLES

Use *a/an* or *the* where needed. If no article is needed, write an X in the blank space.

Only _____ few decades ago, _____ renovation was unpopular and generally far more expensive than taking down _____ abandoned building and starting from _____ beginning. _____ change began in _____ 1960s with _____ number of _____ well-advertised projects. They included _____ Ghirardelli Square in _____ San Francisco, where _____ old chocolate factory was restored and made into _____ shops and _____ restaurants; _____ Trolley Square in _____ Salt Lake City, where _____ abandoned car warehouses became _____ shopping mall; _____ Soho district of _____ New York City, where _____ unused warehouses were made into _____ artists' studios and _____ apartments.

VI   WORD FORMS

	verbs	nouns	adjectives and participles	adverbs
A.		privacy	private	privately
B.		eagerness	eager	eagerly
C.	centralize	center	central	centrally
D.		expense	expensive inexpensive	expensively
E.		history	historic	historically
F.	construct	construction	constructive destructive	constructively
G.		desire	desirable undesirable	
H.	imagine	imagination	imaginative unimaginative	imaginatively

Use the correct word in the sentences below.

A. privacy, private, privately
1. George is not a very sociable person; he likes his _____.
2. He lives very _____.

3. Many people think _____ schools in America are better than public schools.

B. eagerness, eager, eagerly
1. We _____ awaited the news of Mary's trip.
2. We were _____ to know what she did.
3. If she had known about our _____, she would have written sooner.

C. centralize, center, central, centrally
1. This store is convenient because it is _____ located.
2. It is right in the _____ of town.
3. New York City has _____ the control of its public schools.
4. The _____ office is located in Brooklyn.

D. expense, expensive, inexpensive, expensively
1. These shoes were _____ because I got them on sale.
2. Usually, they are much more _____.
3. Sarah's house is _____ decorated.
4. She will go to any _____ to improve the appearance of her house.

E. history, historic, historically
1. When you visit _____ places, you can learn a lot about _____.
2. New York City is a _____ interesting place.

F. construct, construction, constructive, destructive, constructively
1. You should make _____ suggestions when people ask you to criticize their work.
2. If your suggestions are _____, they won't ask for your advice any more.
3. George always gives advice _____.
4. The city is planning to _____ a new building on that site.
5. The _____ should take about a year.

G. desire, desirable, undesirable
1. I have always had a _____ to live in New York City.
2. I think it is a very _____ place to live.
3. True, some neighborhoods are _____ because of the crime.

H. imagine, imagination, imaginative, unimaginative, imaginatively
1. Children usually have a good _____.
2. They are very _____.
3. Adults are usually _____, compared to children.
4. Can you _____ what life will be like in 100 years?
5. I just read a book about football that was _____ written.

VII VALUES DISCUSSION

Answer the following questions. Then discuss your answers with your classmates.

1. How do you feel about old buildings compared to new buildings?
   a. Old buildings are better.

b. New buildings are better.
c. I have no preference.
d. other

2. What is the best reason to renovate an old building?
   a. It is very attractive on the outside.
   b. It is cheaper than building a new one.
   c. It shows respect for the past.
   d. other

3. How do people in your native country feel about old, historic buildings?
   a. They love old buildings.
   b. They dislike old buildings.
   c. They don't care.
   d. other

4. How do you think most people in the United States feel about old buildings?
   a. They love old buildings.
   b. They dislike old buildings.
   c. They don't care.
   d. other

5. How important is it, in your opinion, to preserve old buildings?
   a. very important
   b. not important—it doesn't matter
   c. It is better to build new buildings.
   d. other

6. How do you feel about "renovation neighborhoods" (areas where people are fixing up old, run-down houses)?
   a. They are probably good places to live.
   b. They are probably bad places to live.
   c. I wouldn't want to live there and fix up an old house.
   d. other

7. How do you feel about "community spirit" (people caring about their neighbors, trying to keep the neighborhood clean and safe, and so on)?
   a. It is very important.
   b. It is not important.
   c. I only care about my family.
   d. other

8. How much community spirit exists where you live now?
   a. a lot of community spirit
   b. no community spirit
   c. enough community spirit
   d. other

9. How much community spirit exists in your native country compared to in the United States?

    a. There is more in my native country.
    b. There is more in the United States.
    c. The same amount exists in both places.
    d. other

10. How do you feel about "nostalgia" (thinking about how good things were in the past)?
    a. It is good.
    b. It is bad.
    c. I never feel that.
    d. other

VIII ROLEPLAYING

Choose one of the following situations to act out.

1. An architect is explaining to a reporter why it is sometimes good to renovate old buildings.
2. A person is going to move into an apartment building that used to be an abandoned factory. The person is explaining to a friend how he or she feels about this.
3. A city planner is explaining to a group (which can be the whole class) the advantages of renovating old buildings. The group can then ask questions.
4. A builder is telling an investor why he or she should renovate an old building that the investor has just bought. The investor would prefer to build a new building.
5. A person who likes old buildings is arguing with someone who prefers new buildings about which kind of building is better.
6. A neighborhood resident is telling a reporter how he or she feels about a beautiful old building that may be torn down.
7. A person who just moved into a renovation neighborhood (area where people are fixing up old, run-down houses) is telling a friend why he or she likes living there. (For example, the house is big and inexpensive, there is community spirit, and so on.)
8. A real estate agent is telling a married couple why they should move into a renovation neighborhood, even though many of the houses are old and run-down.
9. A person who lives in an area with no community spirit is giving a reporter reasons for not liking this area.
10. A person who lives in an area with a lot of community spirit is giving a reporter reasons for liking this area.

IX FOR DISCUSSION AND COMPOSITION

Choose one of the following to discuss or write about.

1. What are some advantages of renovating an old building rather than building a new one?
2. Do you know of a case where an old, run-down building was renovated? If so, tell what happened. (Where is it? What was it like before renovation? When was it renovated? Why? What is it like now?)
3. How do people in your country feel about old, historic buildings? Discuss with examples.
4. Describe an area, either in the United States or in your native country, that has a lot of beautiful old buildings.
5. Renovation neighborhoods, such as Park Slope in Brooklyn, are places where many people have moved in and fixed up old, run-down buildings. Would you like to live in a place like that? Why?
6. Renovation neighborhoods usually have good community spirit: people know and care about their neighbors, try to keep the neighborhood clean and safe, have block parties, and so on. Describe an area that you know that has good community spirit.
7. In many big city neighborhoods, there is very little community spirit. People usually don't even know other people who live in their own building. Describe an area that you know that has very little community spirit.
8. Is it good for a neighborhood to have community spirit? Why?
9. Compare the amount of community spirit that exists in two different areas (for example, a specific area in the United States and a specific area in your native country or a big city area and a small town area in your native country).
10. "Nostalgia" means thinking about how nice things were in the past. Is it good to be "nostalgic"? Why?
11. Are you a nostalgic person (one who often thinks about how good things were in the past)? Discuss and provide examples.
12. Tell about something that you feel nostalgic about (a very pleasant experience or time in the past that you sometimes think about).

BIG CITIES:
WHY SOME PEOPLE
LEAVE AND SOME
COME BACK

We hear a lot these days about the problems of living in cities: crimes, pollution, crowds, and so on. This article tells about one married couple who grew tired of these problems and left the city, and another couple who grew tired of living in the suburbs° and moved back into
v *the city.*

area outside of a city

1.   Those who decide to move out of cities give two main reasons for wanting to leave: inner-city crime and bad schools. Those who stay, or return from the country or suburbs, are attracted by the convenience of city activities. Two couples discuss their experiences below.

THE LEMONSES

5   2.   It was a difficult decision for Steve and Joyce Lemons to move away from the neighborhood where they both were raised in Chicago. They had hoped to raise their daughters in the same community. About six years ago, the Lemonses began to have doubts about the quality of life in their old neighborhood. Families who had been there
10   for a long time began moving away. Friends disappeared. Many homes were sold. Often they were changed into apartments. Property values decreased as welfare families° and illegal immigrants moved into the neighborhood. Crime increased.

welfare...poor families living on money from the government

Adapted from *U.S. News & World Report* (April 5, 1976).

3. Joyce Lemons explains, "In the last year or so we just became
15 prisoners in our home. We never knew what was going to happen,
there was so much crime in the area. Houses were being burned all the
time. We always had our doors and windows closed and locked."

4. "I kept asking myself," says Steve, "why work like a dog every day
only to come home and lock yourself up in your home? I never knew
20 what to expect in the neighborhood, and I was always worried about
my family's safety. I was getting an ulcer° from living in constant fear."

sore, damaged area in the stomach

5. In June 1975, the Lemonses made their decision. They bought a
home twenty-five miles outside the city. It is located on several acres° of
land, which Joyce calls "our own small corner of the world where no
25 one bothers us." The house payments are three times more than the city
rent but Steve says it's well worth it. Also, he is closer to his work. He
adds, "Never under any circumstances° would I move back into the
city. I would change jobs and leave the state first."

area equal to 4000 square meters

under…for any reason

THE COXES

6. When Mr. and Mrs. Edward Cox decided to move into a
30 condominium° on the lake in Chicago, they wondered if this would
make life more difficult for their sons, ages six and ten. The boys were
used to a large house, a yard, a good public school, and friends who all
lived nearby in South Holland, Illinois. The Coxes do not regret their
decision to move. The boys have enjoyed their seven months in
35 Chicago's downtown area. They swim in an outdoor pool at their
building and in a nearby indoor pool in bad weather. They have made
friends quickly, play in the huge° park next to the lake, and take art
classes given at the park. The public school they attend is considered
one of Chicago's best.

an apartment that one owns

very big

40 **7.** Mrs. Cox says she actually feels safer in their new home than in
South Holland, where she was afraid to go out for a walk alone after
dark. "Here, streets are well lighted, and there are always policemen
around," she says. "The fact that people are out at all hours in this area
makes you feel safe." Mr. Cox works at the real estate company° that
45 owns the condominium that the family lives in. He hated commuting°
from South Holland, a ninety-minute drive to his city office.

real…company that sells land
traveling to work

8. Grocery shopping is easier now for Mrs. Cox. A store in the
apartment building fills immediate needs, although prices are a little
high. Costs are more reasonable at a supermarket that is within
50 walking distance. "We sold our second car," says Mrs. Cox. "I walk

everywhere, and so do my sons. I think it's healthy. In the suburbs I was always driving them somewhere. There wasn't much time to develop my own interests." The Coxes find living expenses lower in the city. And both parents have more time to spend with their children. "We
55 feel more like a family now," says Mrs. Cox.

Useful Words and Expressions

introduction
  problems
  cities
  crime
  pollution
  crowds
paragraph 1
  main reasons
  inner-city crime
  bad schools
  stay
  convenience
paragraph 2
  community
  have doubts about
  quality of life
  friends
  disappeared
  property values
  decreased
paragraph 3
  prisoners
  houses
  burned
  doors
  locked
paragraph 4
  kept asking
  work like a dog
  lock yourself up
  worried
  getting an ulcer

paragraph 5
  made their decision
  home
  located
  house payments
  be worth it
  under any circumstances
  move back
paragraph 6
  wondered
  make life difficult
  were used to
  a large house
  made friends
  park
  take art classes
  public school
paragraph 7
  actually
  feels safer
  streets
  well lighted
  real estate company
  hated
  commuting
paragraph 8
  grocery shopping
  easier
  walk
  healthy
  suburbs
  driving
  living expenses
  lower

• • • • •E•X•E•R•C•I•S•E•S• • • • •

I   READING COMPREHENSION

1. What is the main idea of the article?
   a. Big cities are bad places to live.
   b. Some people are happy living in cities and some are not.
   c. There is a lot of crime in cities.

2. People want to live in cities due to
   a. the inner-city crime
   b. the convenience of city activities
   c. the bad schools

3. The Lemonses wanted to stay in their neighborhood because
   a. families began to move away
   b. property values decreased
   c. they were raised in that neighborhood

4. They decided to leave because
   a. they didn't feel safe in the city
   b. the city rent was very expensive
   c. Steve wanted to change jobs

5. Put in the correct order.
   a. It is located on several acres of land, which Joyce calls "our own small corner of the world where nobody bothers us."
   b. They bought a home twenty-five miles outside the city.
   c. In June 1975, the Lemonses made their decision.

6. The Coxes were worried about their sons because
   a. the boys swim in an outdoor pool
   b. the boys play in the park
   c. the boys were used to a large house

7. Mrs. Cox
   a. felt safer where she used to live
   b. feels safer in the city
   c. doesn't go out for a walk after dark

8. Mr. Cox is happy because
   a. he doesn't have to commute anymore
   b. he has a better job
   c. the food prices are cheaper in the city

II VOCABULARY

From the list of words below, choose the correct word for each blank space. Use each word only once.

real estate	commuting	actually
community	main	disappeared
constant	quality	located
wondered	kept	suburbs

1. Those who decide to move out of cities give two _____ reasons for wanting to leave.
2. The Lemonses had hoped to raise their daughters in the same _____ where they were raised.
3. Families who had been there for a long time began moving away. Friends _____.
4. "I _____ asking myself," says Steve, "why work like a dog every day only to come home and lock yourself up in your home?"
5. "I was getting an ulcer from living in _____ fear."
6. Their home is _____ on several acres of land, which Joyce calls "our own small corner of the world."
7. Mrs. Cox says she _____ feels safer in their new home.
8. Mr. Cox works at the _____ company that owns the condominium that the family lives in.
9. He hated _____ from South Holland, a ninety-minute drive to his city office.
10. Mrs. Cox says, "In the _____, I was always driving my children somewhere."

III PREPOSITIONS

Fill in the correct preposition for each blank space.

1. Those who decide to move _____ _____ cities give two main reasons _____ wanting to leave: inner-city crime and bad schools.
2. It was a difficult decision _____ Steve and Joyce Lemons to move _____ _____ the neighborhood where they both were raised _____ Chicago.
3. About six years ago, the Lemonses began to have doubts _____ the quality _____ life _____ their old neighborhood.
4. "I never knew what to expect _____ the neighborhood, and I was always worried _____ my family's safety. I was getting an ulcer _____ living _____ constant fear.
5. When Mr. and Mrs. Edward Cox decided to move _____ a condominium _____ the lake _____ Chicago, they wondered if this would make life more difficult _____ their sons.

6. The boys swim _____ an outdoor pool _____ their building and _____ a nearby indoor pool _____ bad weather.
7. Mrs. Cox feels safer _____ their new home than _____ South Holland, where she was afraid to go _____ _____ a walk _____ dark.
8. Mr. Cox works _____ the real estate company that owns the condominium that the family lives _____. He hated commuting _____ South Holland, a ninety-minute drive _____ his city office.

IV   COMMON EXPRESSIONS

Choose the correct expression for each blank space.

worth it	property values	like a dog
have doubts about	under any circumstances	getting an ulcer
made friends	were used to	make life difficult
living expenses	take art classes	made their decision

1. About six years ago, the Lemonses began to _____ the quality of life in their old neighborhood.
2. _____ decreased as welfare families and illegal immigrants moved into the neighborhood.
3. "I kept asking myself," says Steve, "why work _____ every day only to come home and lock yourself up in your home?"
4. In June 1975, the Lemonses _____ to move.
5. The house payments are three times more than the city rent but Steve says it's well _____.
6. He adds, "Never _____ would I move back into the city."
7. The Coxes wondered if moving would _____ for their sons.
8. Their sons _____ a large house, a yard, a good public school, and friends who all lived nearby.
9. The boys _____ given at the park.
10. The Coxes find _____ lower in the city.

V   DEFINITE/INDEFINITE ARTICLES

Use *a/an* or *the* where needed. If no article is needed, write an X in the blank space.

It was _____ difficult decision for Steve and Joyce Lemons to move away from _____ neighborhood where they both were raised in _____ Chicago. They had hoped to raise their daughters in _____ same community. About six years ago, _____ Lemonses began to have _____ doubts about _____ quality of _____ life in their old neighborhood. _____ families who had been there for _____ long time began moving away. _____ friends disappeared. Many homes were sold. Often they were changed into _____ apartments. _____ property values decreased as _____ welfare families and _____ illegal immigrants moved into _____ neighborhood. _____ crime increased.

VI   WORD FORMS

verbs	nouns	adjectives and participles	adverbs
A. inconvenience	convenience	convenient inconvenient	conveniently
B. appear disappear	appearance disappearance	apparent	apparently
C.	neighbor neighborhood	neighborly	
D. change	change	changing	
E. legalize	legality	legal illegal	legally illegally
F. explain	explanation	explanatory	
G. imprison	prison imprisonment prisoner	imprisoned	
H. save	safety	safe unsafe	safely

Use the correct word in the sentences below.

A. inconvenience, convenience, convenient, inconvenient, conveniently
   1. This supermarket is very _____ located for me.
   2. I'm glad it has such a _____ location.
   3. The _____ of shopping is a good thing about city living.
   4. I hope it won't _____ you to see me tomorrow.
   5. If it is _____, we can make another appointment.

B. appear, disappear, appearance, disappearance, apparent, apparently
   1. First the rabbit was there, and then the magician made it _____.
   2. It was not at all _____ how he did the trick.
   3. The rabbit's _____ surprised the audience.
   4. Sam _____ to be a good worker.
   5. _____, he has been doing this kind of work for a long time.
   6. Be careful about your _____ when you go to a job interview.

C. neighbor, neighborhood, neighborly
   1. George is a good _____.
   2. He has always been very _____ to me.
   3. He has been living in this _____ for ten years.

D. change, change, changing
   1. There have been many _____ in education in the past few years.
   2. _____ methods are improving education.
   3. It is difficult for old teachers to _____ their ways.

E. legalize, legality, legal, illegal, legally, illegally
   1. You had better not park there; it's _____.

2. If you park _____, you won't get a ticket.
3. The _____ of George's action is in question; if a judge decides it was not _____, he will have to pay a fine.
4. Many people come into the United States _____.
5. Some people in the United States want to _____ the use of marijuana.

F. explain, explanation, explanatory
   1. Thank you for your very clear _____.
   2. The _____ notes in this book aren't very good.
   3. My teacher said he didn't have time to _____ this to me.

G. imprison, prison, imprisonment, prisoner, imprisoned.
   1. The _____ escaped from _____ last night.
   2. He had been _____ for burglary.
   3. Many countries _____ people who are opposed to the government.
   4. _____ for political reasons is less common in the United States than in many other countries.

H. save, safety, safe, unsafe, safely
   1. This is not a good neighborhood; people don't feel _____ here.
   2. They can't walk in the streets _____ at night.
   3. When people feel _____ in a neighborhood, they usually want to move.
   4. It is terrible to always have to worry about your _____.
   5. You can _____ a lot of money by shopping carefully.

VII VALUES DISCUSSION

Answer the following questions. Then discuss your answers with your classmates.

1. How do you feel about cities?
   a. They are good places to live.
   b. They are bad places to live.
   c. They are bad for most people who live there.
   d. other

2. What is the worst thing about living in cities?
   a. crime
   b. crowds
   c. unfriendly people
   d. other

3. What is the best thing about living in cities?
   a. You don't have to commute to work.
   b. There are interesting activities. (movies, restaurants, and so on)
   c. Nobody cares what you do.
   d. other

4. What is the best thing about living in the suburbs?
   a. You have more room. (a big house or a yard, for example)
   b. The schools are good.
   c. There isn't so much crime.
   d. other

5. What is the worst thing about living in the suburbs?
   a. You have to commute to work.
   b. All the people are the same.
   c. You have to go everywhere by car.
   d. other

6. Are cities good places for children?
   a. yes
   b. no
   c. sometimes
   d. other

7. Schools in cities are
   a. good
   b. bad
   c. usually bad
   d. other

8. What would you look for first in deciding to move to a new area?
   a. an apartment with a low rent
   b. a neighborhood with pretty houses
   c. good schools
   d. other

9. If you could live anywhere, where would you live?
   a. in a city
   b. in the suburbs
   c. in the country
   d. other

10. The nicest place I have ever lived is
    a. in a city
    b. in a small town
    c. in the country
    d. other

11. Most people live in cities because
    a. their jobs are there
    b. they like the interesting activities
    c. they find the people who live there interesting
    d. other

12. How would you compare cities in the United States and in your native country?
    a. Cities in my native country are nicer.

b. Cities in the United States are nicer.
c. They are the same.
d. other

VIII ROLEPLAYING

Choose one of the following situations to act out.

1. The Lemonses are explaining to their two daughters why they have to move out of the city.
2. Mr. and Mrs. Lemons are discussing how they feel about having to move out of their old neighborhood in the city.
3. Mr. Lemons is telling a friend at work why he moved out of the city.
4. Mrs. Lemons is telling a new neighbor why she moved out of the city.
5. Mr. and Mrs. Cox are discussing how they feel about moving back into the city.
6. Mr. and Mrs. Cox's two boys are telling their parents how they feel about living in the city.
7. Mr. Cox is telling a friend at work why he likes living in the city.
8. Mrs. Cox is telling a neighbor in her new building why she likes living in the city.
9. A real estate agent is trying to rent the Lemons's old apartment to a young married couple. The couple are asking questions about the neighborhood.
10. A real estate agent is trying to sell the Cox's old house to a young married couple, who are asking questions about the disadvantages of living so far from the city.
11. A reporter is talking to a group of people who live in a city "slum" (poor, run-down neighborhood) about why they dislike living there.
12. A reporter is talking to a group of people who live in a very nice city neighborhood about why they like living there.

IX FOR DISCUSSION AND COMPOSITION

Choose one of the following to discuss or write about.

1. Why do some people move out of cities?
2. Why do some people want to live in cities?
3. Discuss some advantages and disadvantages of living in cities.
4. Explain why the Lemonses decided to leave the city.
5. Explain why the Coxes moved back into the city.
6. What do the Coxes like about living in the city.
7. Describe a slum (poor, run-down) area of a city either in the United States or in your native country. Why do people dislike living there?
8. Describe a very nice area of a city either in the United States or in your native country. Why do people enjoy living there?

9. Discuss some advantages and disadvantages of living in the country (an area with few houses and a lot of open land).
10. Describe an area in a city where you have lived or now live. What did you (do you) like and dislike about it?
11. Describe an area outside a city where you have lived or now live. What did you (do you) like and dislike about it?
12. If you could live anywhere, where would you live (in a city, in the suburbs, in the country, in a small town)? Why?

THE MEDIA

NEW POPULARITY FOR MOVIES: WHAT'S BEHIND THE COMEBACK?

Movies makers feared for a while that they might be put out of business by television. Recently however, more and more people have been going to the movies. This may be partly because the economic situation in America has become worse. In the movies, you forget your
v *troubles as you get involved in the story on the screen. Also, directors have been producing pictures that large numbers of people want to see.*

1.   Americans by the millions are returning to a love affair with the movies. Motion picture industry experts see two main reasons for this: an increased need by Americans to escape from economic worries and a large number of new movies with broad audience appeal.

5   2.   Credit for the new creativity goes to an active new school of men and women behind the cameras: the directors. They are the artists who rescued° the films from their difficulties—and possibly death at the   saved
hands of television. One actor with experience in both movies and T.V. observes, "The real excitement today is on the theater screen—and not
10 the boob tube° at home where everything has to be simplified for the   **boob**...negative word for T.V.
smallest mind. Something had to be done to force people out of their armchairs, and the directors did it." Films such as "The Godfather," parts one and two, and "The Towering Inferno" have attracted large audiences to movie houses which used to be nearly empty. Good
15 scripts° are more important than ever, with action and laughs still the   written plays
two qualities most in demand.

Adapted from *U.S. News & World Report* (March 17, 1975).

3. Movie makers admit that their rising popularity is partly the result of poor economic conditions, which traditionally bring an increase in theater attendance. "When people are fearful about the future, they look for escape," comments Jack Valenti, president of the Motion Picture Association of America. "In a darkened theater, with a 65-foot screen, you lose yourself° for two and a half hours. People find this beneficial." Sociologists compare the trend° with that of the Great Depression of the 1930s when the movie industry was one of the few businesses that did well. A number of critics consider that period— when some of the greatest film comedies, adventures, and musicals were made—as the golden age of the cinema.

lose...stop thinking about yourself
general direction of development

4. Under somewhat similar circumstances, according to film scholars, the industry now is entering another era° of greatness. The new "stars," however, are often the directors, and not the performers such as Clark Gable and Jean Harlow, who reigned° in Hollywood four decades ago. With a freedom rarely granted by the studios° before World War II, directors are leaving such a clear mark on their works that, in some cases, they are about as well known as the actors they employ. Among the new directorial "giants": Francis Ford Coppola, who made "The Godfather," Peter Bogdanovich, whose works include "The Last Picture Show" and "Paper Moon," and Stanley Kubrik of "A Clockwork Orange" fame. Influencing today's movie makers are the surviving elements of widespread experimentation in the 1960s. Images and sounds intended to shock—including violence, sex, and improper language rare° on the screen before 1960—also have been included in current productions.

time
ruled, led
companies that make movies
unusual

5. Peter Bogdanovich is a writer-director who emphasizes "good stories." He believes that some of the recent "disaster"° movies about such things as fires and earthquakes are "not terribly good" but have attracted large audiences because they offer interesting plots.° One of his movies, "The Last Picture Show," tells about the closing of a small-town theater and the end of an age of innocence. The movie, released in 1971, is widely regarded as influential in establishing a new direction in films. The production combined old-fashioned story telling with honest realism.

terrible accident
stories

6. Increasingly over the past few years, producers have concentrated on love stories with widespread appeal at a time when affection in real life often seems to be absent. Themes° include not only traditional man-and-woman romances but also platonic friendships° between men and even ties between human beings and animals. One story— described by its makers as "not a conventional° picture"—was "Harry and Tonto." It is about a man traveling around the country with a cat, finding that change is good. Paul Mazursky, who directed and helped

subjects
platonic...
nonphysical relationships
normal, average

write the picture, says it illustrates the strength of the new system under
60 which a director picks and develops his own subjects. The rule
previously was that studios assigned stories to directors under
contract,° whether they liked the idea or not.

legal agreement

7. There is widespread agreement that films from now on will be
more critical and less innocent than in the past—reflecting a maturing
65 of Americans in recent wars, political scandals, and economic troubles.
Jack Valenti of the Motion Picture Association predicts, "There's a
chance we will enter a whole new era of creativeness because of new
audiences for the movies."

Useful Words and Expressions

introduction
  movie makers
  out of business
  television
  going to the movies
  economic situation
  forget your troubles
paragraph 1
  love affair
  experts
  reasons
  escape
  appeal
paragraph 2
  credit
  directors
  rescued
  excitement
  theater screen
  boob tube
  something had to be done
  action
  laughs
  in demand
paragraph 3
  popularity
  economic conditions
  traditionally
  lose yourself
  beneficial

trend
  the Great Depression
  the golden age
paragraph 4
  era of greatness
  freedom
  images
  shock
  violence
  sex
  improper language
paragraph 5
  good stories
  disaster
  fires
  earthquakes
  interesting plots
  old-fashioned
  story telling
  realism
paragraph 6
  love stories
  affection
  absent
  themes
  romances
  platonic friendships
  conventional
  director
  his own subjects

under contract   less innocent
paragraph 7   maturing
   widespread agreement   wars
   from now on   political scandals
   critical   economic troubles

• • • • •E•X•E•R•C•I•S•E•S• • • • • •

I   READING COMPREHENSION

1. What is the main idea of the article?
   a. Americans like television more than movies.
   b. More people are going to movies these days.
   c. America has economic worries.

2. One of the reasons for the increasing popularity of movies is
   a. a need to escape from problems
   b. a new group of actors and actresses
   c. interesting T.V. programs

3. The "boob tube" (line 11) refers to
   a. movies
   b. television
   c. the theater screen

4. What does not happen in a darkened theater?
   a. You lose yourself for two and a half hours.
   b. You can escape from problems.
   c. You think about your problems.

5. What is not true about directors today?
   a. They leave a clear mark on their works.
   b. They are always less well known than actors.
   c. They are the new stars.

6. According to Peter Bogdanovich
   a. the recent disaster movies are good
   b. the disaster movies have not attracted large audiences
   c. good stories are important in movies

7. What is not true about Paul Mazursky?
   a. He directed "Harry and Tonto."

b. He likes to pick his own subjects.

c. He likes his studio to give him subjects.

8. Put in the correct order.

a. A number of critics consider that period the golden age of the cinema.

b. Sociologists compare the trend with that of the Great Depression of the 1930s when the movie industry was one of the few businesses that did well.

c. Movie makers admit that their rising popularity is partly a result of poor economic conditions.

II   VOCABULARY

From the list of words below, choose the correct word for each blank space. Use each word only once.

disaster	rescued	screen
experts	trend	themes
shock	widespread	traditionally
conventional	escape	contract

1. Motion picture industry _____ see two main reasons for the growing popularity of movies: a need by Americans to _____ from economic worries and new movies with broad audience appeal.

2. The directors are the artists·who _____ the films from their difficulties.

3. The real excitement today is on the theater_____.

4. Sociologists compare the _____ with that of the Great Depression of the 1930s.

5. Images and sounds intended to _____ have also been included in current productions.

6. _____ include not only traditional man-and-woman romances but also platonic friendships between men.

7. One story—described by its makers as "not a _____ picture"—was "Harry and Tonto."

8. The rule previously was that studios assigned stories to directors under _____ whether they liked the idea or not.

9. There is _____ agreement that films from now on will be more critical and less innocent.

III   PREPOSITIONS

Fill in the correct preposition for each blank space.

1. Americans _____ the millions are returning _____ a love affair _____ the movies.

2. Motion picture industry experts see two main reasons _____ this: an increased need _____ Americans to escape _____ economic worries and a large number _____ movies _____ broad audience appeal.

3. _____ a darkened theater, _____ a 65-foot screen, you lose yourself _____ two and a half hours.

4. _____ a freedom rarely granted _____ the studio _____ World War II, directors are leaving a clear mark _____ their works.

5. One _____ Bodganovich's movies, "The Last Picture Show," tells _____ the closing _____ a smalltown theater and the end _____ an age _____ innocence.

6. Increasingly _____ the past few years, producers have concentrated _____ love stories _____ a time when affection _____ real life often seems to be absent.

7. "Harry and Tonto" is _____ a man traveling _____ the country _____ a cat.

8. There's a chance we will enter a whole new era _____ creativeness because _____ new audiences _____ the movies.

IV COMMON EXPRESSIONS

Choose the correct expression for each blank space.

lose yourself	love affair	economic conditions
boob tube	the golden age	from now on
old-fashioned	love stories	improper language
platonic friendships	in demand	had to be done

1. Americans by the millions are returning to a *love affair* with the movies.
2. The real excitement today is on the theater screen—and not the *boob tube* at home.
3. Something *had to be done* to force people out of their armchairs.
4. Good scripts are more important than ever, with action and laughs still the two qualities most *in demand*.
5. In a darkened theater, you *lose yourself* for two and a half hours.
6. A number of critics consider the period of the Great Depression *the golden age* of the cinema.
7. "The Last Picture Show" combined *old-fashioned* story telling with honest realism.
8. Producers have concentrated on *love stories* at a time when affection in real life often seems to be absent.
9. Themes include not only traditional man-and-woman romances but also *platonic* _____ between men. *friendships*
10. Films *from now on* will be more critical and less innocent than in the past.

V   DEFINITE/INDEFINITE ARTICLES

Use *a/an* or *the* where needed. If no article is needed, write an X in the blank space.

_____X_____ movie makers admit that their rising popularity is partly __the__ result of _____X_____ poor economic conditions, which traditionally bring __an__ increase in _____X_____ theater attendance. "When people are fearful about __the__ future, they look for __X__ escape," comments Jack Valenti, president of __the__ Motion Picture Association of __X__ America. "In __a__ darkened theater, with __a__ 65-foot screen, you lose yourself for two and __a__ half hours. __X__ people find this beneficial."

VI   WORD FORMS

verbs	nouns	adjectives and participles	adverbs
A.	art		
	artist	artistic	artistically
B. simplify	simplicity	simple	simply
C.	innocence	innocent	innocently
D.	realism	real	realistically
	realist	realistic	
		unrealistic	
E.	tradition	traditional	traditionally
		nontraditional	
F. describe	description	descriptive	
G. agree	agreement	agreeable	
	disagreement	disagreeable	
H. criticize	criticism	critical	critically
	critic		

Use the correct word in the sentences below.

A. art, artist, artistic, artistically
   1. John wants to be an __artist__ when he grows up.
   2. He has always been very __artistically__
   3. Making good movies is an __art__.
   4. The movie I saw last night was __artistic__ directed.
B. simplify, simplicity, simple, simply
   1. Programs on T.V. are often very __simply__.
   2. Writers try to __simplify__ them in order to attract a large audience.
   3. __Simplicity__ is often good.
   4. If you speak __simple__, you will probably be understood.

C. innocence, innocent, innocently
  1. The _innocent_ man was unjustly sent to prison.
  2. He hopes to prove his _innocence_.
  3. He says he was _innocently_ walking by the scene of the crime when the police arrested him.

D. realism, realist, real, realistic, unrealistic, realistically
  1. Peter Bogdanovich believes that films should be _realistic_; he is a _unrealistic_.
  2. _realism_ in films is a new trend; people want to see movies about _real_ life.
  3. _realistically_, we will need a week to do this work; to think we can do it in three days is _realist_.

E. tradition, traditional, nontraditional, traditionally
  1. _tradition_, in many societies, men work outside the house and women stay home.
  2. Many women today want to change this _traditional_
  3. They don't want to marry men who are too _nontraditional_
  4. These _traditional_ ideas sometimes cause trouble in marriages.

F. describe, description, descriptive
  1. The writer _describe_ the town where he grew up in his novel.
  2. His _description_ was extemely interesting.
  3. Critics praised the _descriptive_ details in the book.

G. agree, agreement, disagreement, agreeable, disagreeable
  1. John and James can't seem to come to an _agreement_.
  2. Personally, I _agree_ with James's point of view.
  3. John has many _disagreement_ with people.
  4. In fact, he can be a very _agreeable_ person.
  5. On the other hand, his sister Mary is quite _disagreeable_.

H. criticize, criticism, critic, critical, critically
  1. Mr. Roberts is a well-known movie _critic_.
  2. He was very _critic_ of the movie he discussed last night.
  3. _criticism_ can help an artist to look at his work _critically_.
  4. You should always try to _criticize_ someone's work constructively.

VII VALUES DISCUSSION

Answer the following questions. Then discuss your answers with your classmates.

  1. How do you feel about going to movies?
    a. It is a good way to spend time.
    b. It is not a good way to spend time.
    c. It is good if the movie is very good.
    d. other

  2. What is your favorite kind of movie?
    a. comedies (funny movies)

    b. adventure movies (movies with lots of action)
    c. love stories
    d. other

3. How do you feel about movies compared to television?
    a. Movies are better.
    b. T.V. is better.
    c. They are both the same.
    d. other

4. Are movies a kind of escape?
    a. yes
    b. no
    c. not for me
    d. other

5. What is the best kind of escape from everyday life and its problems?
    a. watching T.V.
    b. a vacation
    c. reading
    d. other

6. How do you feel about American movies?
    a. They are good.
    b. They are not good.
    c. Only the adventure movies are good.
    d. other

7. How do you feel about movies from your native country?
    a. They are good.
    b. They are not good.
    c. Only the love stories are good.
    d. other

8. How often do you see movies?
    a. once a week
    b. once every two weeks.
    c. once a month
    d. other

9. How do you feel about your movie-watching habits?
    a. I see too many movies.
    b. I would like to see more movies.
    c. I would like to see better quality movies.
    d. other

10. How do you feel about violence in movies?
    a. It is good.
    b. It is bad.

    c. It is acceptable if it is related to the story.
    d. other

11. How do you feel about violence on television?
    a. It is good.
    b. It is bad.
    c. It shouldn't be there because of children.
    d. other

12. What is the best pastime?
    a. going to movies
    b. playing a sport
    c. reading a book
    d. other

VIII   ROLEPLAYING

Choose one of the following situations to act out.

1. A typical movie goer is telling a reporter why he or she likes movies.
2. A person who doesn't like to go to the movies is arguing with someone who does about whether going to movies is a good way to spend time.
3. A person who likes realistic movies is arguing with someone who likes unrealistic movies (like "James Bond" movies) about which type of movie is better.
4. A person who just came out of a movie theater is telling a reporter his or her reaction to the movie.
5. A director is telling a reporter what kinds of movies he or she likes to make and why.
6. An actor or actress who prefers to work in the movies is arguing with someone who prefers to work in television.
7. A famous movie actor or actress is telling a reporter the good things and the bad things about being a movie star.
8. A movie critic is telling a reporter what, in his or her opinion, makes a movie good.
9. Jack Valenti (president of the Motion Picture Association of America) is telling a group of people (which can be the whole class) why people go to movies. The group can then ask questions.
10. A person who likes movies better than T.V. is arguing with someone who likes T.V. better than movies.
11. A movie director from your native country is describing the kinds of films that people from your country like.
12. A movie director from your native country is speaking to a reporter and comparing films made in your native country to those made in America.

IX   FOR DISCUSSION AND COMPOSITION

Choose one of the following to discuss or write about.

1. Do you like movies? Why?
2. What is your favorite kind of movie? Why?
3. Tell about a movie that you have seen recently. Did you like it? Why?
4. Tell about the best movie you have ever seen.
5. Which do you prefer, movies or television? Why?
6. Do you agree that movies are a kind of escape? If so, is this good? Why?
7. Discuss another way in which people escape from everyday life and its problems—for example, watching T.V., vacations, reading books, listening to music, drinking, drugs.
8. Do you like American movies? Why?
9. Do you like movies made in your native country? Why?
10. Compare American movies and those made in your native country.
11. Do you approve of violence in movies? Why?
12. What is your favorite pastime—movies, T.V., sports, reading, writing, sitting in cafes, listening to music, visiting friends? Why?

TURNING OFF T.V.: A QUIET HOUR

Robert Mayer

Many people in the United States spend most of their free time watching television. Certainly, there are many worthwhile programs on television, including news, educational programs for children, programs on current social problems, plays, movies, concerts, and so on. Nevertheless, perhaps people should not be spending so much of their time in front of the T.V. Mr. Mayer imagines what we might do if we were forced to find other activities. It might not be such a bad idea!

1.   I would like to propose that for sixty to ninety minutes each evening, right after the early evening news, all television broadcasting° in the United States be prohibited by law.

°sending out programs

2.   Let us take a serious, reasonable look at what the results might be if
5 such a proposal were accepted. Families might use the time for a real family hour. Without the distraction° of T.V., they might sit around together after dinner and actually talk to one another. It is well known that many of our problems—everything, in fact, from the generation gap° to the high divorce rate to some forms of mental illness—are
10 caused at least in part by failure to communicate. We do not tell each other what is disturbing us. The result is emotional difficulty of one kind or another. By using the quiet family hour to discuss our problems, we might get to know each other better, and to like each other better.

°something that takes away one's attention

generation...distance between the young and the old

15 **3.** On evenings when such talk is unnecessary, families could rediscover more active pastimes. Freed from T.V., forced to find their own activities, they might take a ride together to watch the sunset. Or they might take a walk together (remember feet?) and see the neighborhood with fresh, new eyes.

20 **4.** With free time and no T.V., children and adults might rediscover reading. There is more entertainment in a good book than in a month of typical T.V. programming. Educators report that the generation growing up with television can barely write an English sentence, even at the college level. Writing is often learned from reading. A more
25 literate° new generation could be a product of the quiet hour.

able to read and write

5. A different form of reading might also be done, as it was in the past: reading aloud. Few pastimes bring a family closer together than gathering around and listening to mother or father read a good story. The quiet hour could become the story hour. When the quiet hour
30 ends, the T.V. networks might even be forced to come up with better shows in order to get us back from our newly discovered activities.

6. At first glance, the idea of an hour without T.V. seems radical.° What will parents do without the electronic babysitter? How will we spend the time? But it is not radical at all. It has been only twenty-five
35 years since television came to control American free time. Those of us thirty-five and older can remember childhoods without television, spent partly with radio—which at least involved the listener's imagination—but also with reading, learning, talking, playing games, inventing new activities. It wasn't that difficult. Honest. The truth is
40 we had a ball.°

extreme, very different

had...had a very good time, enjoyed ourselves

Useful Words and Expressions

introduction	right after
free time	television broadcasting
watching television	prohibited
worthwhile	*paragraph 2*
news	take a look at
educational programs	distraction of T.V.
social problems	together
plays	one another
movies	well known
concerts	problems
other activities	in fact
paragraph 1	generation gap
propose	divorce rate

mental illness
communicate
disturbing
emotional difficulty
get to know
paragraph 3
  pastimes
  take a ride
  take a walk
paragraph 4
  reading
  growing up
  barely
  write an English sentence
  college level
  literate
paragraph 5
  reading aloud

a good story
better shows
get us back
paragraph 6
  at first glance
  radical
  the electronic babysitter
  control
  free time
  remember
  radio
  involved
  imagination
  learning
  talking
  playing games
  have a ball

• • • • •E•X•E•R•C•I•S•E•S• • • • •

I READING COMPREHENSION

1. What is the main idea of the article?
   a. In the past, people didn't watch television.
   b. We should show no television programs for about one hour every evening.
   c. Television improves our lives.

2. The failure to talk to each other causes all of the following except
   a. a real family hour
   b. the generation gap
   c. some forms of mental illness

3. If we turned off T.V. for an hour
   a. we would not have any problems
   b. there would be a higher divorce rate
   c. families could take a ride together

4. According to the author
   a. T.V. is more entertaining than books
   b. books are as entertaining as T.V.
   c. books are more entertaining than T.V.

5. Because we don't read much
    a. T.V. is very entertaining
    b. even college students can't write well
    c. writing is learned from reading

6. The idea of an hour without T.V. is not radical because
    a. T.V. is only twenty-five years old
    b. T.V. is an electronic babysitter
    c. we might get better shows

7. Life without T.V.
    a. used to be very difficult
    b. used to be a lot of fun
    c. wasn't good for children's imaginations

8. Put in the correct order.
    a. By using the quiet family hour to discuss our problems, we might get to know each other better, and to like each other better.
    b. The result is emotional difficulty of one kind or another.
    c. We do not tell each other what is disturbing us.

II VOCABULARY

From the list of words below, choose the correct word for each blank space. Use each word only once.

barely	pastimes	radical
distraction	remember	disturbing
emotional	together	involved
prohibited	story	babysitter

1. I would like to propose that for sixty to ninety minutes each evening, all television broadcasting in the United States be _____ by law.
2. Without the _____ of T.V., families might sit around together after dinner and actually talk to one another.
3. We do not tell each other what is _____ us. The result is _____ difficulty of one kind or another.
4. On evenings when talking over problems is unnecessary, we might rediscover more active _____.
5. Educators report that the generation growing up with television can _____ write an English sentence.
6. Few pastimes bring a family closer together than gathering around and listening to mother and father read a good _____.
7. At first glance, the idea of an hour without T.V. seems _____.
8. Those of us thirty-five and older can _____ childhoods without television, spent partly with radio—which at least _____ the

listener's imagination—but also with reading, learning, talking, playing games, inventing new activities.

III   PREPOSITIONS

Fill in the correct preposition for each blank space.

1. I would like to propose that _____ sixty _____ ninety minutes each evening, right _____ the early evening news, all television broadcasting _____ the United States be prohibited _____ law.
2. Without the distraction _____ T.V., families might sit together _____ dinner and actually talk _____ one another.
3. Many _____ our problems—everything, _____ fact, _____ the generation gap to some forms _____ mental illness—are caused _____ least _____ part _____ failure to communicate.
4. There is more entertainment _____ a good book than _____ a month _____ typical T.V. programming.
5. Educators report that the generation growing _____ _____ television can barely write an English sentence, even _____ the college level.
6. When the quiet hour ends, the T.V. networks might even be forced to come _____ _____ better shows _____ order to get us _____ _____ our newly discovered activities.
7. _____ first glance, the idea _____ an hour _____ T.V. seems radical.
8. Those _____ us thirty-five and older can remember childhoods _____ television, spent partly _____ radio—which _____ least involved the listener's imagination—but also _____ reading, learning, talking, playing games, inventing new activities.

IV   COMMON EXPRESSIONS

Choose the correct expression for each blank space.

get to know	get us back	growing up
right after	take a look at	one another
well known	in fact	take a ride
at first glance	college level	free time

1. Let us _____ what the results might be if a quiet hour were required.
2. Families might sit around together after dinner and actually talk to _____.
3. It is _____ that many of our problems—everything, _____, from the generation gap to the high divorce rate, are caused at least in part by failure to communicate.
4. By using the quiet family hour to discuss our problems, we might _____ each other better.

5. Families might _____ together to watch the sunset.
6. Educators report that the generation _____ with television can barely write an English sentence, even at the _____.
7. _____, the idea of an hour without T.V. seems radical.
8. It has been only twenty-five years since television came to control American _____.

V   DEFINITE/INDEFINITE ARTICLES

Use *a/an* or *the* where needed. If no article is needed, write an X in the blank space.

With _____ free time and _____ no T.V., _____ children and _____ adults might rediscover _____ reading. There is _____ more entertainment in _____ good book than in _____ month of _____ typical T.V. programming. _____ educators report that _____ generation growing up with _____ television can barely write _____ English sentence, even at _____ college level. _____ writing is often learned from _____ reading. _____ more literate generation could be _____ product of _____ quiet hour.

VI   WORD FORMS

verbs	nouns	adjectives and participles	adverbs
A. prohibit	prohibition	prohibited	
B. accept	acceptance	acceptable	acceptably
		unacceptable	
C. distract	distraction	distracted	
		distracting	
D. talk	talk	talkative	
E.	emotion	emotional	emotionally
		unemotional	
F. act	activity	active	actively
	actor		
	actress		
G.	child	childish	childishly
	childhood		
H.	honesty	honest	honestly
		dishonest	

Use the correct word in the sentences below.

A. prohibit, prohibition, prohibited
   1. Many people have suggested the _____ of cigarettes.
   2. If we _____ cigarettes, maybe fewer people will get lung cancer.

3. It is _____ for minors (persons under eighteen) to buy cigarettes in the United States.

B. accept, acceptance, acceptable, unacceptable, acceptably
1. I appreciate your _____ of my suggestion.
2. I didn't know if you would _____ it.
3. If you had found it _____, I would have been disappointed.
4. The clothes that John wore to the dinner were _____; he was _____ dressed.

C. distract, distraction, distracted, distracting
1. I find it _____ to study and listen to the radio at the same time.
2. The radio is a _____ for me.
3. It _____ me from paying attention to my work.
4. When I am _____, I can't work well.

D. talk, talk, talkative
1. Sally is a very _____ person; she _____ too much.
2. I enjoyed Dr. Brown's _____ on the state of the economy last night.

E. emotion, emotional, unemotional, emotionally
1. Men do not seem to be as _____ as women.
2. That is because they are taught not to show their _____.
3. Sometimes it is an advantage to be _____, for example, at work.
4. If you react very _____ to your boss at work, you could get in trouble.

F. act, activity, actor, actress, active, actively
1. Although Jack Lemmon is an excellent comic _____, he can also play serious roles.
2. Jane Fonda is one of the best _____ in the United States.
3. I used to _____ in plays when I was in college.
4. Bike riding is a healthy _____.
5. It is good for old people to be _____ involved in their communities.
6. When old people are _____, their health usually improves.

G. child, childhood, childish, childishly
1. _____ is usually a happy time of life.
2. Many people wish they were a_____ again.
3. George was behaving very _____ at the party last night.
4. He apologized today for being so _____.

H. honesty, honest, dishonest, honestly
1. I wouldn't go into business with Sam if I were you; I think he is _____.
2. I _____ think you would be making a mistake if you did that.
3. I like _____ people.
4. _____ is a great virtue.

VII   VALUES DISCUSSION

Answer the following questions. Then discuss your answers with your classmates.

1. What do you think of Mr. Mayer's proposal to turn off T.V. for sixty to ninety minutes every night?
    a. It is a good idea.
    b. It is a bad idea.
    c. It would be good to try it.
    d. other

2. What would be the greatest advantage of turning off T.V. for an hour every night?
    a. People would talk to each other more.
    b. People would spend more time outside.
    c. People would read more.
    d. other

3. How do you feel about television?
    a. It is good.
    b. It is bad.
    c. People watch it too much.
    d. other

4. What is the best thing about television?
    a. It gives people something to do.
    b. It keeps young people off the streets.
    c. It informs you about what is happening in the world.
    d. other

5. How much time do you spend watching T.V. every night?
    a. one hour
    b. two hours
    c. three hours
    d. other

6. How do you feel about the amount of time you spend watching T.V.?
    a. I spend too much time watching T.V.
    b. I spend just enough time watching T.V.
    c. I would like to spend more time watching T.V.
    d. other

7. What is your favorite kind of T.V. program?
    a. police stories
    b. comedies
    c. news
    d. other

8. What do you think of the television watching habits of people in your native country (what they watch, how much T.V. they watch) compared to those of people in the United States?
    a. The people in my native country have better habits.
    b. The people in the United States have better habits.

c. People in the United States watch more, but the programs are better.
d. other

9. How do you feel about the way in which people communicate with each other?
   a. People don't communicate enough.
   b. There is nothing wrong with the way people communicate.
   c. People talk to each other, but they aren't really friendly.
   d. other

10. How do you feel about "therapy" (seeing a psychologist or therapist to talk about problems) as a way to help people communicate better?
    a. It is a good thing to do.
    b. It doesn't help.
    c. People should talk to their friends instead.
    d. other

11. What do you think about using T.V. as an electronic babysitter for children?
    a. It is a bad thing to do.
    b. There is nothing wrong with that.
    c. People don't do that.
    d. other

12. What do you think about violence on T.V.?
    a. There is too much violence.
    b. The amount of violence is not bad.
    c. I would like to see more violence.
    d. other

VIII ROLEPLAYING

Choose one of the following situations to act out.

1. A parent is explaining to a child why it is bad to watch too much television.
2. Mr. Mayer (or a female speaker) is explaining to a group (which can be the whole class) why television should be prohibited for one hour every night. The group can then ask questions.
3. Television has been prohibited for one hour every night. A family (father, mother, one or two children) are discussing what they are going to do for this hour.
4. A person who dislikes T.V. is arguing with someone who likes it about the advantages and disadvantages of watching T.V.
5. A person is telling a reporter why he or she never watches T.V.
6. A person is explaining to a reporter why he or she spends a lot of free time watching T.V.
7. A person whose career involves helping people to communicate (a therapist, counselor, marriage counselor, group leader) is telling a reporter (or a group of people) why it is important to communicate.

8. A person who feels that T.V. is used too much as an "electronic babysitter" is arguing with someone who disagrees.
9. Two people who disagree about whether there should be violence on T.V. are arguing.

IX FOR DISCUSSION AND COMPOSITION

Choose one of the following to discuss or write about.

1. What would be some advantages of turning television off for an hour every night?
2. Discuss the advantages and disadvantages of watching T.V.
3. Do you think people watch too much T.V.? Discuss with examples.
4. Do you watch too much T.V.? Discuss with examples.
5. What kinds of programs do you like to watch on T.V.? Why?
6. Describe the television-watching habits of people in your native country or in the United States—for example, when they watch T.V., what they watch, how much they watch, and so on.
7. Do you think that people do not communicate enough? Discuss with examples.
8. What are the negative effects of people failing to communicate with each other?
9. Discuss one or more ways to help people learn to communicate with each other better.
10. Do you feel that television is used too much as an "electronic babysitter"? Discuss with examples.
11. Do you feel that there is too much violence on T.V.? Why?
12. Do you think people used to be happier before television existed? Why?

WORD LIST

Following is a list of all words used in the articles, and the page and paragraph in which each word first occurs (2-3 means page 2, paragraph 3; 2-t means page 2, title; and 2-i means page 2, introduction). Asterisks (*) indicate words that are glossed (g.), or words that occur in the exercises on vocabulary (v.) or word forms (w.). Expressions that are glossed or found in the common expressions exercises (c.) are indented. Page numbers of exercises where the words occur are indicated. Numbers, months, days of the week, and names of people and places are omitted. If necessary, a word's part of speech is indicated (verb, *v*; noun, *n*; adjective, *adj*; adverb, *adv*).

a 3-i
*abandoned g. 121-1
able 25-i
about 4-2
absent 148-6
*academic g. 14-3
*accept 110-3, w. 164
according to 14-2
account 38-5
ache 74-5
achieve 49-1
*acre g. 134-5
*action 15-8, w. 164
   acting out c. 41
*actually 134-7, v. 137
addition 14-4
*administrator g. 14-4

*admire 97-4, w. 102
admit 148-3
*adult g. 13-t
advantage 73-i
*adventure 73-1, w. 79
advertise 122-2
advice 61-i
affair 147-1
affection 148-6
*afford 49-1, v. 77
afraid 134-7
after 13-i
against 62-A4
age 15-7
   the aged c. 29
*agency g. 13-1
ago 3-1

*agree 97-i, w. 153
ahead 14-5
*alimony g. 109-2
all 3-1
   at all c. 102
allow 4-2
*alone 25-i, v. 52
along 86-4
aloud 160-5
already 4-3
also 4-5
alternative 26-3
*although 26-3, v. 112
always 26-3
among 14-6
amount 62-A2
and 4-2

animal 38-5
another 3-i
answer 75-8
anyone 73-1
anything 61-A1
apartment 121-1
*appear 15-10, w. 139
application 38-3
*appointment 85-3, v. 88
appreciate 121-i
approach 37-i
*architect g. 121-1
area 121-i
*argue 62-A3, w. 68
armchair 147-2
around 3-i
*arrange 85-3, v. 88
arrive 3-i
*art 4-4, w. 153
article 97-i
artist 122-2
as 3-i
   as far as c. 7
   as well as c. 19
ashtray 86-5
ask 49-i
   assembly line g. 75-7
*assertive g. 98-8, v. 100
assign 149-6
association 15-7
at 4-3
attend 15-8
*attention v. 52
attentive 14-3
attitude 110-3
*attract 15-8, w. 19
audience 147-2
authority 61-t
automobile 63-A2
*available 61-A1, v. 65
average 62-A5
*avoid 110-4, v. 112
*aware 97-3, v. 100
away 25-i

baby 49-i
babysitting 86-5
back 13-i
background 109-1
*backpacking g. 14-6
bad 15-10

bank 38-5
barber 3-1
*barely 160-4, v. 162
basically 62-A4
   back to basics g. 37-2,
    c. 41
be 1-i
because 13-i
become 4-2
bed 25-1
before 25-2
begin 4-2
   from the beginning c. 125
behind 3-1
believe 14-3
belly dancing 14-6
belong 85-1
*benefit g. 75-8, v. 77
best 63-A2
better 3-1
between 25-2
big 14-4
bill 14-2
bird 3-1
bit 122-3
   boob tube g. 147-2, c. 152
book 160-4
bookkeeping 37-1
*boring g. 14-5
both 15-10
*bother 86-5, v. 88
boy 3-1
bread 62-A4
break 4-5
bring 148-3
broad 147-1
*broadcasting g. 159-1
brother 4-4
build 50-3
building 121-t
burn 134-3
business 3-1
   go out of business c. 7
busy 98-6
but 3-1
buy 50-3
by 13-1

can 3-1
call 25-2
*calorie g. 63-top

camera 147-2
campaign 121-1
*campus g. 14-2
cancer 61-i
car 15-8
carcinogens 62-A1
*care 14-6, w. 30
career 14-4
case 74-3
cat 148-6
*catalogue g. 14-6
cause 4-5
*celebrate g. 4-4
*center 13-i, w. 126
cereal 62-A1
certain 61-i
chance 50-4
   a 50-50 chance c. 53
   by chance c. 89
*change 15-8, w. 139
   changed into c. 125
character 122-4
*charity g. 25-1
cheap 25-1
chemicals 61-i
chemist 4-3
*child 3-1, w. 164
chocolate 122-2
*choice 25-2, v. 28
chop 63-A4
church 4-2
cinema 148-3
circumstances 134-5
   under any circumstances
    g. 134-5, c. 138
citizen 49-2
city 15-8
class 14-2
classmate 15-10
classroom 13-1
clean 85-i
clearly 85-2
*clinic g. 74-6
close *adj* 14-3
clothes 85-i
clothing 121-1
coffee 86-5
college 4-4
   college level c. 163
*colon g. 62-A1
color 62-A3
combine 148-5

*legal 133-2, w. 139
 less 4-3
 lesson 98-4
 let's 62-A5
 level 13-1
*liberation 49-1, w. 54
*lie 25-1, v. 28
 life 3-1
   life expectancy g. 74-4
 lifelong 13-i
 life style 49-i
 light *v* 134-7
 like 4-3
 like *v* 4-3
 likely 62-top
 line 15-8
 list 14-6
 listen 98-8
 liter 4-2
*literate g. 160-4
 little 3-1
*live 3-i, w. 30
   living expenses c. 138
 local 13-1
*locate 15-8, v. 137
*lock 3-1, v. 6
*lonely 25-1, v. 28
 long 25-2
   before long c. 78
 look 26-3
   look good c. 66
*loser g. 26-4, w. 90
   lose yourself g. 148-3,
     c. 152
 lot 38-2
 love 38-5
   love affair c. 152
   love stories c. 152
 low 74-4
 lunch 26-3

 machine 38-5
*main 133-1, v. 137
*maintain g. 63-A4
 major 4-5
 make 3-1
   make life difficult c. 138
   make sure g. 26-3, c. 89
   make use of c. 41
   made little effort c. 19
   made the decision c. 138

 male 85-2
*mall g. 122-2
 man 62-A5
*manage 86-3, v. 88
 many 3-i
 mark 148-5
 marriage 49-2
*marry 3-1, w. 8
 masculine 98-8
 material 122-4
 mathematics 38-5
 mature 14-3
 may 98-5
 maybe 25-1
 me 3-1
 meal 86-4
 mean 3-i
 mechanic 38-5
 medical 73-1
   medical staff g. 75-7
*medicare g. 26-4
*medicine 75-6, w. 79
 meditation 14-6
 meet 25-1
 member 14-7
 mend 85-i
 mental 159-2
 mention 62-Q5
*menu 86-4, v. 88
*method g. 37-1, v. 40
 middle 74-4
 midway 37-1
 might 62-Q5
 mile 134-5
 milk 4-2
 mind 147-2
 mine 85-2
 minerals 63-top
 minister 110-4
 minute 159-1
*miss 73-1, v. 77
   missing out on g. 97-2
 model 121-1
 modern 61-i
*mold g. 62-A4
 money 26-4
 month 3-1
 more 3-1
   more and more c. 113
   more than c. 125
 morning 25-1
 most 3-i

 most important of all
   c. 29
 mother 85-1
 motion picture 147-1
 motorcycle 38-5
 move 3-i
 movies 147-i
 much 15-8
   much of c. 41
 music 148-3
 must 3-1
 my 3-1
 myself 85-3
   by myself c. 89

 nation 13-2
 naturally 86-6
 near 4-3
 nearby 134-6
 necessary 3-i
*need 13-1, w. 19
*neighborhood 15-8, w. 139
 never 4-2
*nevertheless 3-i, v. 6
 new 3-t
 newcomer 4-5
 news 51-i
 next 134-6
 nice 3-1
 night 49-i
 no 4-3
   no longer g. 4-5, c. 7
   no matter c. 125
   no point c. 41
   no way c. 29
 no one 134-5
*normal g. 25-2, v. 40
*nostalgia g. 122-3, v. 124
 not 4-5
 nothing 122-3
 now 3-1
   from now on c. 152
 nowadays 63-A3
 number 13-1
 nursing home g. 25-2
*nut g. 15-10
*nutrition g. 61-t

 object 15-8
*observe 38-2, v. 40

obtain 98-7
*obviously g. 63-A4, v. 65
occasionally 4-5
occur 109-i
of 3-i
off 159-t
offer 13-1
office 26-3
official 14-7
often 25-i
oil 4-5
old 13-i
  old-fashioned 148-5,
    c. 152
*once g. 4-2
one 13-i
  one another c. 163
only 4-2
open 4-3
operate 38-5
*opponents 74-5, v. 77
opportunity 3-i
*oppose w. 79
or 4-3
orange 3-1
order 74-3
*organize 38-6, w. 43
other 4-2
*otherwise 75-7, v. 77
ourselves 62-A4
out 3-1
outside 38-2
over 13-2
overcrowded 50-4
overpopulation 50-4
*overqualified g. 14-5
overweight 61-A2
own *v* 3-1
own *adj* 15-7

pain 74-5
parent 38-6
park 86-3
part 13-2
  in part c. 66
  part-time 13-2, c. 19
*participation 26-3, v. 28
particular 37-1
partner 109-1
pass 86-5
past 14-7

pastime 160-3, v. 162
patient 73-i
pay 3-1
  pay attention to c. 78
peanuts 62-A4
people 3-i
per 62-A5
percent 14-2
perform 148-4
perhaps 63-A4
period 148-3
*person w. 79
  personal experiences 14-3,
    c. 19
  personal relationship c.
    78
pet *n* 38-5
philosophy 14-6
physical 63-A2
piano 121-1
  pick up g. 86-4
picture 61-i
  the pill g. 49-1, c. 53
pity 98-7
place *n* 3-1
plan 14-3
  city planners c. 125
plant 14-6
platonic g. 148-6, c. 152
  platonic friendship
    g. 148-6, c. 152
play *v* 38-5
play *n* 159-i
*playpen g. 26-3
*please 75-7, w. 79
*plot g. 148-5
point *n* 38-2
point *v* 85-i
  point of view c. 53
  to the point where c. 125
policeman 134-7
*political 4-3, w. 8
pollution 133-i
pool 134-6
poor 74-4
popular 14-6
population 14-2
position 98-7
*positive g. 50-5
*possess 4-5, w. 8
*possible 25-i, w. 68
pound 62-A5

poverty 3-i
*power 98-7, w. 103
practical 14-3
practice 38-5
predict 149-7
*prejudice g. 4-5
*prepare 13-i, w. 42
presence 14-3
present *v* 61-i
preserve 62-A2
president 14-3
pretty 62-A4
*prevent 50-4, w. 54
previous 97-i
price 49-1
principle 14-6
*prison 134-3, w. 139
*private 13-1, w. 126
probably 3-1
problem 3-i
*produce 62-A1, w. 114
*professional g. 15-8
professor 14-3
profit 13-2
*program 13-1, v. 28
*prohibit 159-1, v. 162,
  w. 164
*project g. 38-4
promise 3-t
*promotion g. 98-5, v. 100
proof 15-8
*proper 74-4, v. 88
property 133-2
  property values c. 138
propose 159-1
protect 62-A4
proteins 63-top
provide 13-1
psychology 14-6
public 15-8
publications 49-2
pupil 38-4
*purpose 38-6, v. 40
put 73-2

*qualification 38-4, w. 43
quality 4-3
*question 15-7, w. 54
quick 13-2
quiet 159-t

something had to be done
   c. 152
sometimes 15-7
*somewhat 4-5, v. 6
somewhere 50-3
son 135-8
soon 4-5
sound 148-4
   sounds good c. 78
soup 25-1
space 122-4
speak 3-1
*specialist 38-6, w. 90
spend 26-4
   spend time c. 102
sports 98-4
*spread g. 109-1, v. 112
staff 75-7
star 148-4
start 14-4
state 4-2
station 121-1
stay 49-i
steel 4-2
step 14-5
still *adv* 3-t
stomach 62-Q2
stop 13-2
store 38-5
*story 147-i, v. 162
street 134-7
*stress g. 109-i
*strong 4-2, w. 8
structure 122-3
student 13-t
*studio g. 148-4
*study 14-5, w. 42
subject 37-i
substance 62-A1
*suburbs g. 133-i, v. 137
*success 37-i, v. 52, w. 54
such 3-i
sudden 15-7
suffer 3-i
sugar 62-A3
summer 75-7
sunset 160-3
supermarket 61-A1
*support 26-2, w. 90
suppose 13-i
sure 50-5
survive 148-4

*suspect 62-A1, v . 65, w. 67
swim 134-6
*sympathize g. 86-4, v. 88,
   w. 90
*system 4-3, v. 6, w. 8

take 4-4
   take a look at c. 163
   take a ride c. 163
   take art classes c. 138
   take care of c. 29
   take for granted g. 4-5,
     c. 7
   taking down c. 125
*talk 4-2, w. 164
tax 14-6
teach 4-3
*tear *n* 3-1, v. 6
tear *v* 122-3
teens 13-1
teenagers 38-3
teeth 63-top
television 15-8
tell 3-1
*tend 63-Q4, v. 65
*tendency v. 112
tennis 14-6
terrible 61-A1
territory 15-7
test 37-1
text 25-i
than 3-1
that 3-i
the 3-t
theater 148-3
their 3-i
them 4-2
*theme g. 148-6, v. 151
themselves 26-4
then 25-1
*theory g. 15-7, v. 17
therapist 110-4
there 4-3
these 3-i
they 3-i
thing 38-6
*think w. 54
third 13-2
this 3-i
those 3-1
though 73-i

thought 49-1
*threat g. 109-t, w. 102
*threatened g. 98-4, v. 100
   the three R's g. 38-2
through 62-A1
throughout 98-6
throwaway 109-t
thus 50-5
tie 148-6
till 110-3
time 4-4
   a long time c. 113
   all the time c. 66
   at the same time c. 66
   for the first time c. 113
   free time c. 163
   from time to time c. 89
   in time c. 7
tire 133-i
to 3-i
today 4-5
together 110-3
too 4-2
total 25-2
town 3-1
*traditionally 13-1, v. 112,
   w. 153
train *n* 15-8
train *v* 37-t
travel 49-2
treat 74-5
tree 3-1
*trend g. 14-6, v. 151
trip 25-1
trouble 85-i
true 98-7
trust 98-6
try 3-i
turn 3-1
T.V. networks 160-5
type 98-6
typical 61-A1

*ulcer g. 134-4
*undergraduate g. 15-8
*understand 14-5, v. 52
*unemployment v. 17
university 4-3
unless 109-1
until 110-4
up 25-1

PICTURE CREDITS

Chapter

H 7
I 8
J 9